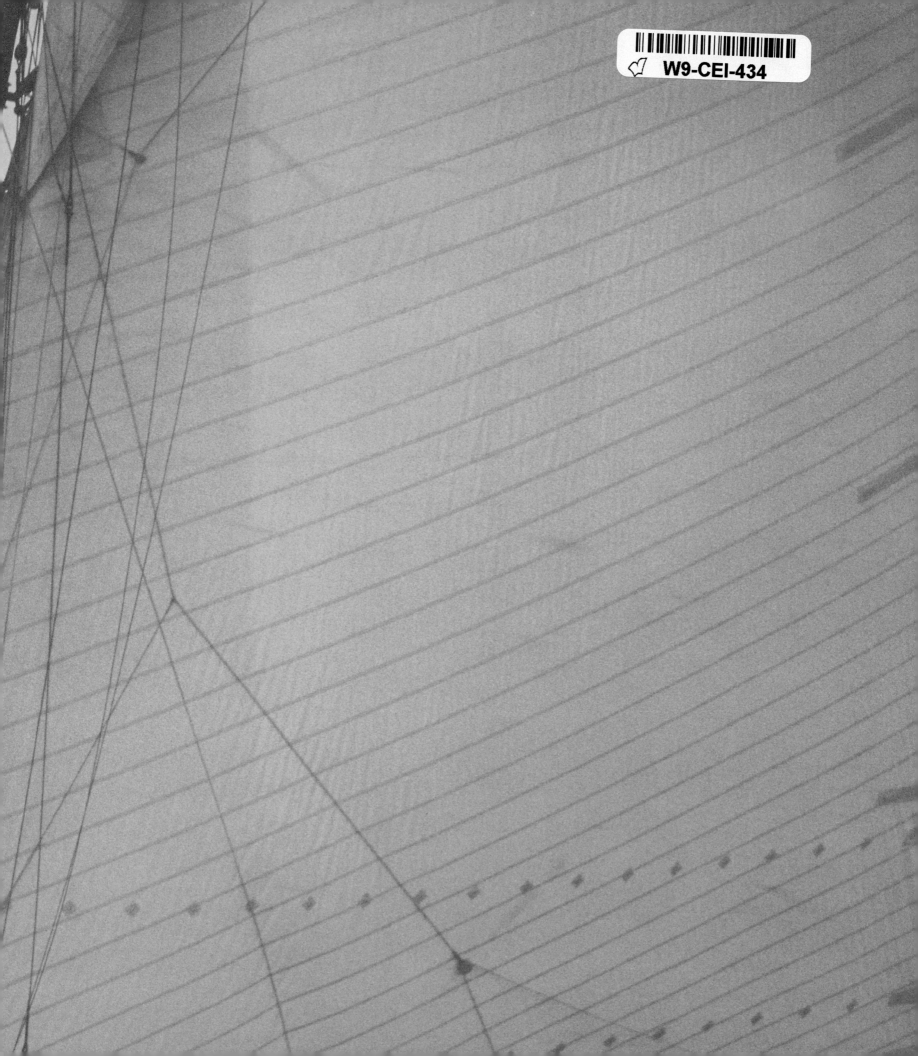

In the
Spirit of Tradition
OLD AND NEW CLASSIC YACHTS

TEXT BY JILL BOBROW

PHOTOGRAPHS BY DANA JINKINS

~

PRODUCED BY CONCEPTS PUBLISHING INC.

W. W. NORTON & COMPANY
NEW YORK · LONDON

For our daughters - Jordan, Quincy, and Sabrina
In these pages we hope to preserve a bit of the past
for the next generation.

Other Books by Jill Bobrow and Dana Jinkins:
Classic Yacht Interiors
The World's Most Extraordinary Yachts
Maxi, The Ultimate Racing Experience
Harbors of Enchantment, A Yachtsman's Anthology
Shenandoah, A Three-Masted Schooner

Library of Congress Cataloging-in-Publication Data
Bobrow, Jill, 1951–
In The Spirit of Tradition : old and new classic yachts / text by
Jill Bobrow : photographs by Dana Jinkins.
    p.   cm.
  ISBN 0-393-04556-0
  1. Yachts.   I. Title.
VM331 . B665   1997
623 . 8 ' 2023—dc21   97–22128

Produced by Concepts Publishing Inc.
P.O. Box 1066
Bridge Street Marketplace
Waitsfield, Vermont 05673
Telephone: (802)496-5580
Telefax: (802)496-5581

W. W. Norton & Company, Inc., 500 Fifth Avenue, New York, N.Y. 10110
W. W. Norton & Company, LTD., 10 Coptic Street, London WCIA IPU

Printed in Hong Kong by Palace Press International

ACKNOWLEDGEMENTS

Photographer: Dana Jinkins
Author: Jill Bobrow
Editor: James Mairs
Editorial Assistant: Susanna McIlwaine
Art Direction/Production: Dana Jinkins
Production Assistant: Bonnie Atwater
Accommodation Plans: Chris Bevington

There are many people we would like to thank including the various people who contributed their thoughts on classics to the first and last sections of this book: Bernard d'Alessandri, Ugo Baravalle, Nathaniel Benjamin, Jol Byerley, Jim Cassidy, William Collier, Ken Coombs, Peter Davies, Virginia Jones, Bruce King, Gary S. Maynard, Iain McAllister, Elizabeth Meyer, John Munford, Eric Pascoli, Rick Steadman, Bob Tiedemann, Duncan Walker, and Hank Wiekens.

Most of the photographs in this book were taken by Dana Jinkins, but in some cases, yacht owners were kind enough to supply us with some necessary photographs that we were missing. We would like to thank contributing photographers: Christophe Baudry, Kip Brundage, Nicolas Clerc, Anne Converse, Robert Douglas, Daniel Forster, Bugsy Gedlek, Sheila Hill, Edward Holt, Richard Imbeault, Kos, Patricia Lascabannes, S. Lindstrom, Leslie Lindeman, Maxwell MacKenzie, Jim Mairs, Christopher Moorhouse, Bill Muncke, Stan Parks, Hervé Rebours, Roy Roberts, Isabelle Rouquette, Sea Island Photography, Peter Swanson, and Ko Wellman.

We would also like to give special thanks to: John Bardon, Harald Baum, Annie Benard, Hersh and Raelea Bobrow, Karla Bove, Christian Chalmin, Boat International Magazine, Fred Croft, John Dwight, Scott and Icy Frantz, Alan and Amy Gowell, Tabitha Griffin, Alice Huisman, Syd Janes, Ed and Sophie Kastelein, Barbara Kranichfeld, Jim Mairs, Glen O'Neil, Sarah Peppercorn, B'fer Roth, Jack Somer, Myrna Snider, Peter Traun, Maguelonne Turcot, and the editors at W. W. Norton & Co.

TABLE OF CONTENTS

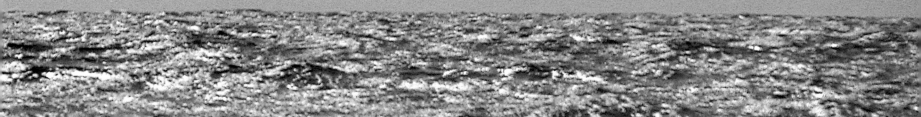

What a vast subject and what a delicate enterprise the authors Jill Bobrow and Dana Jinkins have undertaken over the last ten years! This book is without any doubt the most complete and comprehensive book ever published on classic boats.

There isn't a single definition of a 'classic boat' — even the specialists have different interpretations. By choosing the title *In The Spirit of Tradition*, the authors have demonstrated their true understanding of the subject.

Some classic boats are masterpieces because they have always been cared for and well-maintained, others have become so because they were rescued from rot or neglect and then rebuilt. Now there are even new classics, which have been constructed following traditional design. In all cases, it is the "spirit" of tradition which should be the motivation for all persons (particularly the owners) involved with classic yacht restoration and classic yacht revival. The world of classic boats is tantamount to a philosophy of life.

We should be happy that more and more people recognize and have fallen in love with classic boats and want to participate in saving a culture and preserving historical monuments. Without the dedication of this rarefied group of owners, builders, designers, crafts people, riggers, sail makers, captains and crew, a way of thinking and sailing would have disappeared forever.

ISABELLE ROUQVETTE

Christian Chalmin

Publisher: *Boat International, Mer & Bateaux, Meer & Yachten, The Superyachts* book series—also sponsor, juror, and publisher of numerous classic week events and programs.

Eric Tabarly's Pen Duick *under full sail at the Cannes Régates Royales.*

*W*hen Dana and I produced our first books on yachts, *Classic Yacht Interiors, The World's Most Extraordinary Yachts,* and *Maxi, The Ultimate Racing Experience,* we were trying to meet a broad spectrum of interests. With this new book, we have selected only boats that we personally find intriguing. Having a passion for classic yachts made our job easy.

Passion is key to this book. People sail, buy, restore, and care for classic yachts because they are passionate about them. Otherwise there is no reason to spend the time and money it takes to keep up with a classic yacht. Included in this book are boats that were launched as far back as one hundred years ago, though most were built during the 'golden age of yachting' between the two world wars. Their histories are as rich as the woods from which they were built. These classic yachts transcend their owners; they have lives of their own. People who chose them either took care of their wards—varnished, painted, and refit them when necessary—or, perhaps, neglected them, left them to rot or deteriorate. Whatever transpired over the years, the yachts in this book are survivors. Ultimately, someone nursed them along, repairing, patching, and restoring. In some cases they were

salvaged from the bottom of a river like *Neith*, dredged up from the harbor like *Zaca*, or rescued out of a mud berth like *Avel*. Classic yachts need devoted caretakers.

In the last decade or so, there has been a resurgence in yacht restoration, a desire to preserve the past. The first major classic yacht restoration that Dana and I encountered was *Sheevra*, William Fife's personal yacht that he christened *Clio* in 1921. We photographed her in 1985 at the Veteran Boat Rally in Sardinia for our book *The World's Most Extraordinary Yachts.* The owners —Jeff Law, Don Costanzo, and Olive Adshead—had lovingly

restored this little jewel at Santo Stefano in Italy. Every piece of wood or hardware that could be renewed or recycled into the yacht was. Authenticity was of paramount importance. If they could not execute something just as Fife would have done, they did it in the style of the era. This same team that restored *Sheevra* went on to work with skipper/project manager Paul Goss on the 1931 Fife schooner, *Altair*. For years Dana and I had heard about *Altair*—how she was dismantled to a bare hull, then very carefully restored to her original state in the best possible manner at Southampton Yacht Services in 1986–1987.

The number of boats being restored has accelerated since then. S.Y.S. did a major refit of *Ticonderoga,* and a beautiful job of combining a rebuild with the restoration of a sixty-year-old yacht, *Thendara.* Then *Kentra* and *Fulmar,* two amazing restorations done recently at Fairlie Restorations, set the classic yacht world in Europe all abuzz. The owners of *Kentra* became impassioned about the restoration of their 65-ton cruising vessel—so when *Fulmar,* a Fife 8-meter needed a patron, they decided to rescue her as well!

Fairlie Restorations publishes a credo that says:

Yacht restoration is a process that involves a number of ethical and practical decisions. We feel that compromise is usually a necessity to make a restored yacht comfortable and enjoyable. We feel it may be unreasonable to expect a crew to have no washing or toilet facilities, but perfectly reasonable to want hand-stitched sails. One aspect we are loathe to meddle with is the external appearance of the yachts. We do not feel it is necessary to change fundamental aspects of the design to try and "improve" on the original. At the heart of our company is the belief that, to a large extent, the success of any restoration relies on faith in the original yacht.

Rebuilding a yacht can be close in concept to restoring one, yet there are a host of both distinct and subtle differences. Materials, methods, and design figure in strongly. Gary Maynard, from Martha's Vineyard, is quite articulate on the subject of restoring yachts. With his own boat, *Violet,* he took the

The bow man watches as Altair *jockeys for position at the start in Cannes.*

Tuiga *and* Mariella *racing for the first mark in the Cannes Régates Royales 1996.*

purist approach—"Just keep things the way they were originally." He says, "A classic vessel is a synthesis of proven design principles, traditional technologies, experienced seamanship, and historical continuity. To reject traditional wooden-vessel construction while maintaining a classic aesthetic does no more than create a classic 'look.'" Hans Albrecht, owner of ninety-year-old *Veronique* says, "There is no reason to own a modern boat as it has no soul, no spirit."

It is fortunate that the classic yacht world has people who care deeply. Elizabeth Meyer has made a whole career of rebuilding and restoring yachts (as well as organizing J-Class events), including her own *Endeavour* and her charge, *Shamrock V*. Meyer is also a founding member of the International Yacht Restoration School in Newport, Rhode Island, a not-for-profit organization that teaches the skills, history, and related sciences involved in the restoration of classic yachts.

The owners of *Adela* and *Arawak* have chosen to take their old boats and revamp them, using old and new materials. Carbon-fiber masts on a classic boat? Well. . . it's all possible.

Naval architect Bruce King, who designs modern classics such as *Signe*, *Alejandra*, and *Hetairos*, is quite eloquent on the subject of blending the old with the new and, in fact, has designed many exquisitely beautiful 'new classics.' Patrice de Colmont, one of the primary originators of the famed Nioulargue Race, says, "These boats are not classic…yet; some day they will be."

Steve Hammond, skipper on *Altair*, admires the modern classics—as long as they remain honest about what they are. He would welcome the opportunity to be involved in a yacht-building project that married new technology to an aesthetic ideal. Yet he is incredibly proud of how original *Altair* is after her restoration. She has no hydraulics and is terribly inefficient in many regards, but he believes that changing her to be faster by replacing her full keel with a fin keel and skeg rudder would have been a travesty. Hammond deplores yacht brokers who sell classic boats to inexperienced owners under the premise that their yacht will, like an antique automobile or a fine painting, appreciate in value. He says, "You can't just put a classic yacht in a garage like a car and expect her to maintain her 'good looks.' Classic yachts are a major responsibility for the owner as well as the crew."

All the present-day classic yacht regattas have their own rules and regulations. The Nioulargue committee is very strict about what constitutes a classic—and spirit has everything to do with it. *Adela* was not allowed to race in the Nioulargue as a classic. *Alejandra* was admitted but not as a classic, and the new gaff-rigged schooner *Zaca a te Moana* did race with the classics, with a special rating because she is a modern reincarnation of a turn-of-the-century schooner with a full keel and a heavy displacement. Kenny Coombs and the Antigua Classic Race committee have instituted a new class called "The Spirit of Tradition," from which we borrowed the title of our book. They welcome 'new classics.' The Wooden Boat Series in New England is a relatively new organization, and they seem to be open minded…to a point.

In our book we have chosen to follow our own special criteria. Dana and I both have special feelings about classics, which date back many years. In the late '60s and early '70s, my sister had a 65-foot schooner, built in 1913, on which I participated in schooner races from Essex to Mystic, Connecticut, and all over the Long Island Sound. In the mid '70s, Dana and I met in Bequia in the Grenadines. I had sailed there from the States on the famed Herreshoff ketch *Ticonderoga*, and she arrived via the old Baltic, *Ring Andersen*. The parade of yachts sailing into Admiralty Bay in Bequia was amazing—*Mariette*, *Candida*, *Puritan*, *Harbinger*, *America*, *Escapade*. Throughout the Caribbean there are yachts of every description, but it was invariably the classics that captured our imagination and our hearts.

Both through design and chance, we have followed the classics for years. Seeing a familiar yacht (regardless of who is on it) is like running into an old friend, someone you lost track of in, say, Pulpit Harbor, Maine, but who turns up unexpectedly in Kekova, Turkey. *Belle Aventure* and *Mariella* are two Fifes we have encountered from Antigua to the Côte d'Azur in several incarnations. Where the yachts have been and what they have been through is often an adventure and always a story.

The captain of *Principia* talks about how the grandson of the original owner came aboard unexpectedly and was crestfallen to discover the fireplace his mother reminisced about so often had been removed. The skipper of *Altair* tells the story of the aging son of the blacksmith who worked with Fife coming aboard to see his father's work completed sixty-six years earlier. The people on *Neith* tell a similar tale; it is the same with *Ticonderoga, Zaca,* and most of the others—passersby, men, women, professional people, royalty, celebrities, carpenters, and old crew all recognize the boats from the dock or the harbor and feel a kindred spirit and want to capture a piece of their own past, maybe even their heritage.

Dana and I ventured far to write this book, following classic yacht regattas and events to Maine, Martha's Vineyard, Nantucket, Newport, Antigua, Monte Carlo, Cannes, and St. Tropez, stopping at boatyards and small harbors along the way. We had accumulated a wish list of boats over the years and otherwise relied largely on word of mouth. I interviewed people about a subject they were passionate about and was fascinated by the stories behind these yachts. Dana was excited to be photographing gaff-rigged schooners, ketches, and sloops jockeying for position at the starting lines of numerous regattas. She also loved spending time below, photographing the

sumptuous interiors. But it was not always easy. For the most part the yachts were racing or recuperating, so they were often in disarray or being worked on. Still, our mission was a joyous and fulfilling one.

When we began this book, we had in mind only boats from the past. However, we encountered and were drawn to some very special "new classics." It's inspiring to see the traditional designs still honored and appreciated. We admire authentic restoration and hope that craftsmen never lose the ability to recreate history. Most of the boats in this book are indeed old, and most are wooden; yet some are new, some are composite or steel, some have been restored, others have been replicated or rebuilt. They are all beautiful, and they all have that certain something that renders them classic.

Jill Bobrow

Jill Bobrow

View from the rigging of Mariette.

The varnish, the gaffs, the brass—it is an incredible sight looking through the fleet at the Nioulargue in St. Tropez.

The Wooden Boat Classic Yacht Regatta Series was organized to not only provide benefits to participants and classic regatta organizers, but also to spread the word and zeal about classic boats to those who do not own them.

The series was organized in 1989. With the support of *Wooden Boat* Magazine, this series provided a logical, progression of several classic boat events in the Northeast, from mid-summer through the fall sailing season. Each event has its own unique personality. The races included in the series are: Emperor's Cup, Marblehead Massachussetts; Eggemoggin Reach Regatta, Seven Hundred Acre Island, Maine; Opera House Cup, Nantucket, Massachussetts; Classic Yacht Regatta, Newport, Rhode Island; Governor's Cup, New York City; Race Rock Regatta, Stonington, Connecticut. Each venue preserves its own local identity and as the series is nonprofit, each committee donates the money that is raised to its own special cause.

There are over 400 yachts that participate in the series. These events provide classic boat owners and admirers an unequaled opportunity to gather with those who share their avid interest in owning, preserving and using classic boats. When classic boats gather, at dockside or on the open water, they present a grand spectacle, the appeal of which reaches even those who would not hitherto have considered restoring or owning a classic themselves.

The Wooden Boat Classic Regatta Series brings together classic boats that are virtual legends in the records of yachting history. With sizes ranging from 21 feet to the awesome 120-plus feet of the majestic J Boat, *Shamrock.* There can be, and is, something here for everyone. There is an undeniable difference between owning a modern production boat and owning a master-craftsmen-designed-and-built unique classic boat. Those who participate in, or observe for the first time, any or all of the series' regattas, inevitably do catch the fever, and, in so doing, may acquire, restore, and preserve another of these unique craft. Thus, the Wooden Boat Classic Regatta Series serves to help in the saving of these boats—an irreplaceable testimonial to the talents, skills and labors of the creators.

Jim Cassidy, Mystic Connecticut
Founder, Wooden Boat Series

Page 8: Opera House Cup start; Rugosa *and* Lark.

Spectators gather at the lighthouse to watch the boats come in after the race.

Chips *nearing the finish.*

Pages 10 - 11: Newport Classic Yacht Regatta 1996.
Inserts from top: Fortune; Fleetwing;
and a newly built Alerion.

Camden, Maine, is the homeport of many classic
vessels.

Wooden boat building and repairs are a speciality at
Rockport Marine in Rockport, Maine.

Schooners rafted together in Pulpit Harbor, Maine,
after a summer regatta.

The tenders are as classic as their mother ships.

Spectators watch the Governor's Cup in Boothbay,
Maine.

The Antigua Classic Yacht Regatta was started back in 1988. The Antigua Sailing Week Race committee dropped the classic class because of lack of interest in 1987 and because in 1986, the dying class had only two entries. However, seven large classic yachts turned up in 1988 and had to race in Cruising Class III with the bareboats. It was downright dangerous with the likes of the 114-foot schooner *Ashanti of Saba* on a windward starting line doing 14 knots. After the week had ended, several captains met and decided to hold a different event just for schooners. This was quickly changed to include all classics, and we sailed off to Guadeloupe and back in 1988 with eight yachts. The event has now grown, and we are now celebrating our tenth year, and we expect up to 70 yachts.

The objectives of this event are to gather the beautiful old and new classic yachts together in a celebration of sail without the tight quarters of other racing events, to create a safe spectacle for all the crews and owners to enjoy their vessels in the company of other beautiful yachts, and also to enjoy the ideal sailing conditions here.

Most of us in the yachting scene know a genuine classic when we see one. These yachts have fine lines and acres of canvas, built years ago from wood, with bowsprits and bumpkins, in an age when all yachts were things of beauty and grace. The survivors of this era are unmistakably classic. The Oxford English Dictionary defines 'classic' as something 'of acknowledged excellence' or 'having historic associations.' This includes the restored workboats of the past, which are now plying the seas as yachts. Age is certainly a factor here, but what about when an exact replica is produced using epoxies and other modern materials and keeps the grace and beauty of her predecessor? These yachts must certainly be included, as well. Even new-built yachts that are designed with the grace and style of old classics, with long overhangs, perfect proportions, and fitted out with excellent craftsmanship should be included. A collection of fine yachts—old and new, large and small, fast and slow—come together.

We have several classes in the Antigua Classic Regatta. Vintage Class is for all yachts built before the Second World War, when boat building paused for a while. Classic Class is for all yachts built after the war but still in the traditional way and with original lines and long keels. Schooner Class is especially for schooners and subdivided into like vessels. This brings us to the modern classics, the Spirit of Tradition Class, for those yachts mentioned earlier that have been built to classic lines, maintain the beauty and craftsmanship of the past, but have modern keel and rudder shapes, and use modern or exotic materials. This class is special and it has its own prize structure, so yachts with wing keels and carbon masts can sail against each other and alongside their elder counterparts.

We are committed to the preservation of the skills and craftsmanship that makes the building of these fine ships possible. In 1997 we included a Heritage Tent which housed some exhibits and demonstrations of the traditional boat building methods as well as some of the new. We expect this to grow, and hopefully it will help to make some of the exhibits permanent within the Nelsons Dockyard National Park itself. Plans are also being made to send apprentices to boat-building schools, so they may bring these skills back to Antigua and make Antigua a place to restore or maintain a classic yacht.

We must also pay tribute to the increasing number of owners who are spending the time and money to restore and rebuild the existing classics, keeping them going and preserving them for future generations. Also to those owners who are constructing new-built yachts, taking the time to recreate beautiful yachts that echo the grace and style of the past.

Ken Coombs, English Harbor, Antigua
ACYR Chairman

In the early days of Caribbean chartering, I sailed my two wonderful old wooden yachts through the magical islands of the West Indies. One was the 1928 gaff ketch *Ron of Argyll*. She was as pretty as a picture and as hard mouthed as a Clydesdale stallion. Her teak and oak in the bilge were as well finished as that in the saloon. There were no sharp corners on that boat. I would sometimes spend hours slowly running my hands over her broad, unvarnished teak rail, while my bare toes never tired of the smooth velvety feel of her decks. Because of her, the early 1960s in the charter trade was truly delightful.

Then came *Lord Jim*, one of John Alden's big gaff schooners. For all the years I owned her, I cruised the Caribbean in a state of utter bliss, under gaff topsails, fisherman, and a huge, red-white-and-blue gollywobbler. Of course, I didn't know then that these two yachts would soon be referred to as classics. They were simply just wonderful heaps of wood…and they were actually mine!

I still regularly wake up in the middle of the night having just relived one of the many passages when *Lord Jim*'s glistening bowsprit zeroed in on the high mountains of the next island. The splendid old schooner loved it as much as I, and together we were the king and queen of the Caribbean.

No fiberglass or steel vessel could ever talk to me as she could, and at the end of the day I would usually paddle out in the dinghy and in the soft West Indian twilight simply gaze with satisfaction at my beautiful ship. Both *Ron of Argyll* and *Lord Jim* defined the word 'classic'.

Jol Byerley, English Harbor, Antigua
Nicholson's Caribbean Yacht Sales

Jol Byerley, English Harbor, Antigua.

The fleet attending the Antigua Classic Yacht Regatta docked in Falmouth Harbor.

Summer Cloud, *built in Carriacou.*

Page 16–17 inserts: Alzavola *leads the fleet to the first mark.*
Vileehi.
Ticonderoga *and* Fleurtje.
Mariella *and* Hetairos.

The Monaco Classic Week is the main event organized by the Yacht Club de Monaco. It is a time of festivities and the celebration of classic yachts, not just a racing week. It is magical to see motor yachts and powerboats, from the beginning of the century and up to the 1950s, side by side with traditional sailing yachts. Exhibitions and demonstrations, classic sailing yacht challenges and other trials, competitions of elegance, history, and technical contests occur throughout the week. Cocktail parties, dinners, presentations, and award ceremonies are also organized around the event and contribute to making the week exceptional.

We are very proud of our maritime heritage, and the main purpose of the occasion is to perpetuate a long seafaring tradition—and to illustrate and convey the rich history of Monaco and of these wonderful boats—to all participants and spectators, particularly the younger generation. Through this pageant, the Yacht Club de Monaco hopes also to sustain the interest of owners, professionals, and amateurs alike, and all people who may eventually contribute to the preservation of these magnificent yachts. There is no doubt that without their devotion, these boats would no longer survive today, and part of the maritime history of Monaco would also tragically disappear with them.

Each year the event is organized around a main theme. In 1996 the Yacht Club de Monaco succeeded in bringing together most of the existing Fife designs still surviving today. A spectacular affair!

The year 1997 was exceptional for the principality, as it celebrated the 700th anniversary of the Grimaldi dynasty. As a fitting tribute to its princes, Monaco staged numerous events throughout the year, centered around its history. Of course, this included a very special Monaco Classic Week, with, as a main theme, some of the amazing Tall Ships.

All are welcome, and in the Yacht Club de Monaco's relentless search for traditional and classic yachts, all are invited to submit entries for sailing yachts, motor yachts and powerboats, which are accepted under strict criteria such as authenticity, original restorations, and, of course, beauty.

Bernard D'Alessandri
Director, Yacht Club de Monaco

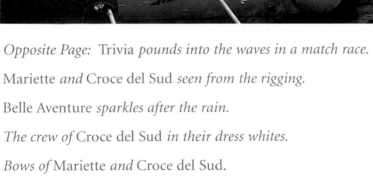

Opposite Page: Trivia *pounds into the waves in a match race.*

Mariette *and* Croce del Sud *seen from the rigging.*

Belle Aventure *sparkles after the rain.*

The crew of Croce del Sud *in their dress whites.*

Bows of Mariette *and* Croce del Sud.

Fulmar *reefed down for some strong wind.*

Monaco Classic Week is a fun-filled event which includes an extraordinary collection of boats, exhibits along the quay, as well as competitions for both sailing yachts and powerboats.

The Cannes Régates Royales is held every year, the week before the Nioulargue. The last race is a feeder race to St. Tropez.

The yachts lined up stern-to in the old part of Cannes create a breath-taking spectacle.

Jockeying for position before the start of the first race.

Mariette and Zaca a te Moana.

The Nioulargue had its inception in September 1981 when Jean Lorrain on *Ikra* and Dick Jayson on *Pride* decided to engage in a race from Portalet to the Club 55 passing to seaward around the "Nioulargue" (a submerged rock five miles off Pampelonne Beach; in Provençal the word means spawning ground for fish). The race was a success for both participants and spectators. The celebration party after the race laid the groundwork for the future. The Nioulargue has grown over sixteen years to be the most popular end-of-season sailing event in the Mediterranean.

Yacht owners or their representatives from all around the world write to the Nioulargue committee asking to be accepted as a competitor in our regatta. We know many of them personally, others by reputation, and some not at all. Our decision on who is eligible is based largely on 'spirit.' We started the Nioulargue in 1981 with just two boats, *Ikra* and *Pride*—of course, competition is competition, but most importantly the race is meant to be fun!

For several months of the year, St. Tropez is the center of the world—all the boats want to come here…and why not? Early on, during the first years of the Nioulargue, there was a large odd-looking research-type vessel which belonged to an influential businessman. The captain wanted to enter her in the Nioulargue, but the committee rejected the boat. The businessman was not used to being refused anything. After a short period of time, I received a phone call from the Chamber of Commerce asking me to convince the committee to reconsider. We wouldn't. Next we got a call from the Secretary General of the Prefect who tried to pressure us to accept the boat. Still, we had our standards, and we did not want to accept her because she (and the owner) did not have the right spirit. The saga did not end there—the next plea on behalf of this persistent man came from the Minister of the Interior! I spoke to the Minister and explained how we had a small harbor, limited dock space, a full roster of boats, and no particular desire to include this particular boat no matter how much money and influence the owner had. Nevertheless, I suggested that if the Minister was so intent on getting her accepted then we would allow her, but some other yacht that was already signed up would have to be removed from the list. We invited the Minister to choose a boat from the list and tell the owner why his place was being usurped. The boat in question did not race that year (nor any other year).

A classic yacht is a boat that has a life already—a history—it does not have to be made of wood and does not have to be an antique. Some maxis are classics—*Wallygator* is a classic—newly-built traditional looking boats are not classic yet, but in time they will become classic. To be a classic yacht, and to race in the Nioulargue as a classic, there are technical criteria, but above all, the owner must have the Corinthian Spirit! The following credo is printed in French on the *inside* of M. de Colmont's sweatshirt (next to his heart).

The Corinthian Spirit and the Classic Yachtsman are one. The Corinthian Spirit is a philosophy of life.
One can recognize it both ashore or at sea. It doesn't just mean fair play—moreover, it cannot be explained, or justified, cannot be demonstrated—nevertheless, its presence is manifested in certain ways:

1) To be discreet and modest in victory or defeat.
2) To remain courteous in the most desperate maneuvers.
3) To have style, but not so much as to be arrogant.
4) To show good will, as it is infectious.
5) Never to forget that the regatta is for fun and must remain so...
6)…

Patrice de Colmont, St. Tropez
Proprietor of Le Club 55
President of the Nioulargue Organization Committee

Aerial view of St. Tropez from the spreaders of Thendara.

The town fire boat gets involved with the customary evening water fight.

The yacht crew costume parade.

In June of 1996, Brittany's major port was closed for one week to all vessels of war and trade. For that week, the harbor was packed with 2500 classic craft at the world's largest maritime festival. Due to their sheer magnitude, tall ships predominated, especially *Swan*, the world's largest barquentine (200 feet). Still, most of the boats were small—over half were under 26 feet—canoes rigged with lugsails, also cobbles, punts, and dinghies.

Over four million people came to Brest to watch the racing and partake of the merriment. There were over 2000 musicians on hand, theater and exhibits depicting maritime themes, and boats and boats and more boats. A highlight was La Régate Brest-Douarnenez. At least 30 boats over 100 feet participated and many more spectators—the horizon was cluttered with lateens, square sails, luggers, gaffs, and jackyard topsails. Brest '96 was a classic event of major proportion.

Stan Parks
Sailor, Photographer, owner of classic yachts

BREST PHOTOGRAPHS BY HERVE REBOURS AND STAN PARKS

Type: Schooner
LOA: 169' (51.50 m)
LOD: 139' (42.40 m)
LWL: 99' (30.20 m)
Beam: 25' 11" (7.90 m)
Draft: 15' 9" (4.85 m)
Displacement: 230 tons
Hull: Steel
Designer: Gerry Dijkstra
Builder: Fay & Co.; Southampton, England
Restoration: Pendennis Shipyard;
    Falmouth, England
Year built: 1903; rebuilt 1995
Engine: 1 x 640 hp Lugger 6-170A diesel

A D E L A

Adela is an extraordinary yacht in every sense of the word; she is very old, very big—169 feet—very beautiful, very fast, *and* she is one of the most controversial classic yachts afloat today.

This grand yacht started life as a William Storey schooner called *Heart Seas.* Built in steel and wood in 1903 by Fay's of Southampton, England, for Claude Thornton Cayley, she was awarded a special cup by the German kaiser soon after her launching for being one of the finest schooners afloat. Cayley cruised her extensively until World War I, at which time he sold her. She was later discovered much deteriorated near Brightlingsea on the east coast of England, with her masts removed and her lead ballast stripped. Her story is not dissimilar from that of Gucci's *Avel;* both sailing yachts ended up as houseboats languishing in mud berths, forgotten and forsaken. A valiant attempt to resurrect *Adela* was initiated in 1971; a 30-ton steel keel replaced her cast-lead keel, and she was given a three-masted rig. However, her refit was underfunded, and the attempt was aborted.

It was not until 1992, when she was purchased by an American businessman who had owned several other sailing boats, that a true renascence began. Filled with flotation airbags, she was towed from Lowestoft to the Pendennis Shipyard in Falmouth. At the yard she was thoroughly surveyed, and it was determined that all the structural steel and most of the wood planking would have to be replaced. Naval architect Gerry Dijkstra was hired to redraw the underwater lines and work with Pendennis to develop a game plan. The teak hull had deteriorated irreparably, so the owner and the yard decided to rebuild her in steel. A fin and skeg underbody was grafted on to accommodate easier maneuverability. This was just the beginning; in the end vir-

tually the whole boat was rebuilt: new decks, new engine room, new superstructure, new accommodation plan, new rig. Still, the profile and freeboard above the waterline retains the same vestige of the old boat, and some parts of the original styling were recreated or incorporated where possible.

The interior of *Adela* is exquisite. From the deckhouse on down the companionway to the cabins and the main saloon, you are immersed in a maze of gorgeous Cuban and African mahogany. The owner's stateroom is situated in what used to be called the "ladies cabin" because that was where the least motion was, making it the refuge of preference for those prone to seasickness. This stateroom, as with virtually all the interior, was rebuilt. However, original marble and silver-plated fittings were retained in the bathroom. The guest cabin to port is the only original cabin onboard; this space was used as a mold from which Pendennis matched the joinery work throughout the boat. Small things such as light fittings and finger switches were salvaged from the old boat as was an old decorative chart box. The entire interior design was fashioned after the Edwardian period; paneling, furniture, and furnishings were all thoroughly researched.

It is not the interior or the expansive new teak deck, not even the superstructures or new-fangled hardware, that have caused controversy for *Adela*. All her modern peculiarities might have been overlooked if it weren't for her incredible rig, which has been expanded to accommodate the extra weight of her tanks, engine, generators, et cetera. Her spars and boom are carbon fiber, and her main mast is a staggering 160 feet high. Her modern North Sails-built Spectra array includes quadrilateral flying jib, stay sail, foresail, and huge mainsail with a gaff foresail. There are 24,295 square feet of sail that require a veritable army of crew to race the boat. She is incredibly fast and has a wonderful steady motion at sea. Right after her debut in her new configuration in the south of France

in 1995, she attempted to enter the world-famous Nioulargue race as a classic but was not allowed to participate as a restored classic. Purists complain that she was not restored as she should have been, and some say that her original hull was destroyed. Others feel that her underbody and rig are inappropriately modern. Still others feel that the owner should have had the prerogative to rebuild her any way he wanted to, pointing out that the owner salvaged all that was not beyond repair. In Antigua at the Classic Yacht Regatta of 1996, she raced in the class called Spirit of Tradition with other new classics, such as *Alejandra* and *Hetairos*. With all of her high-tech gear and rig she had the appropriate high-tech sailor at the helm, none other than Dennis Conner! The Antigua Classic Yacht Regatta is not the America's Cup, and *Adela* is not a restoration—but she is extraordinary!

page 30– The teak deck is interrupted only by stainless-steel fittings and 35 hydraulic Lewmar winches.

The deck saloon has cupboards cleverly hiding all of the modern electronics.

Page 31– The main saloon is richly paneled in mahogany.

The master stateroom has a queen-size bed, a sitting area, and an en suite bath.

Type: Yawl
LOA: 82' (25.02 m)
LWL: 59' 6"(18.13 m)
Beam: 14' 6"(4.42 m)
Draft: 9' 10"(3.00 m)
Displacement: 35.8 metric tons
Hull: Mahogany
Designer: Knud H. Reimers
Builder: B. Plym; Stockholm, Sweden
Restoration: Cantieri Carlini; Rimini, Italy
Year built: 1948, rebuilt 1988
Engines: Fiat AIFO 180-ch

A G N E T A

Agneta was designed by Swiss naval architect Knud Reimers to be his personal yacht and constructed by the Plym Boatyard in Stockholm in 1948. Reimers named the boat after his daughter. Due to ill health and other circumstances, he kept the boat only a few years. In 1952 well-known Italian businessman Gianni Agnelli bought her. He sailed her and loved her for twenty-five years. In 1981 she was bought by Count Donà Delle Rose, who kept her near his home in Porto Rotundo, Sardinia.

Agneta's life took a significant turn in 1987 when Italian architect Giuseppe Andolina bought her and proceeded to rebuild and restore her. The work was done at the Carlini yard in Rimini. Everything from the hull on up was rebuilt, and her original Marconi yawl rig was restored. The most startling changes took place in the interior accommodation. Her varnished hull had always been impressive to passersby, but very few people could ever have imagined what was below. The entire original interior was dismantled. The accommodation belowdecks now boasts a veritable symphony of wood: teak, pear, spruce, and mahogany. (Andolina found a trunk of African mahogany that was 12 meters long and 2.5 meters in diameter.) Before any of the interior was built, each piece was created in a mock-up.

The fireplace in the main saloon was recreated three times. A single fine woodworker toiled for a year and a half creating the interior space. In fact 18,000 hours are recorded in total for the work time spent on the renovation of *Agneta*. The effect is a dazzling display of brightwork; solid wood is curved, carved, inlaid, and laminated. In contrast to—and the only relief from—the imposing wood are the stained glass panels, mirrors, upholstered settee, and carefully selected objets d'art. The owner's stateroom is as opulent as the main saloon. The en suite bathroom is an exten-

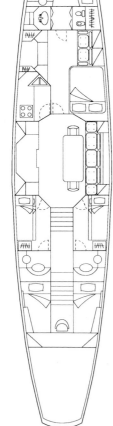

sion of the rest of the interior, fitted with inlaid floors and marble.

Agneta belongs today to Andolina's widow, Raffaella Stefani. In 1993, a few weeks before the Nioulargue Race, Gianni Agnelli took the opportunity to revisit his beloved *Agneta*. He was effusive and warm in congratulating Raffaella on the stunning new interior that her husband had masterminded. For Raffaella, the boat has practically become her raison d'être. She says, "*Agneta* has a spirit, a spirit of all the things that I have loved during all of these years." She feels that all the energy, hard work, and vision her husband expended on recreating *Agneta* has paid off. *Agneta* is elegant and fast and responds well in light air as well as in heavy weather. Raffaella races her hard and loves being involved in all aspects of the boat. She claims that *Agneta* has given back the joy in her life.

The master bath is a veritable symphony of wood and marble.

The master cabin has a cozy atmosphere. There is a double bed and separate lounge area with a couch faced by a charming fireplace.

Murano stained glass adorns the cabinets in the main saloon and arched bookshelves are a theme from the saloon to the cabins.

Type: Ketch
LOA: 135' 6" (41.34 m)
LWL: 100' (30.50 m)
Beam: 26' 4" (8.04 m)
Draft: 12' 6" (3.85 m)
Displacement: 170 tons
Hull: Aluminum
Designer: Bruce King Yacht Design
Builder: Mefasa Shipyard; Avilés, Spain
Year built: 1993
Engine: Single MTU 12 V183 Type TE62

ALEJANDRA

Alejandra is incredibly beautiful and combines most definitely extraordinary classic lines with sophisticated, up-to-date technology. She was the first yacht that naval architect Bruce King was responsible for in its entirety. King's name is associated with some of the most romantic yachts in existence today, *Whitehawk, Whitefin, Signe,* and *Sophie* to name a few. There is no question that King has a classic approach, but he bends and augments the parameters. The man who commissioned *Alejandra* to be built had previously owned *Whitefin.* According to Steve McLaren, project manager and skipper of *Alejandra,* the owner was ready for a larger yacht with a more expansive and formal interior. Still, despite an extraordinary interior accommodation, the designer's brief was to create a yacht from the exterior; thus the result is low freeboard with maximum curvature to the sheer (which is in fact accentuated with a recessed waistline and cove stripe). The decks are clean and uncluttered with a low profile and a discreet deckhouse. Hatches are flush mounted into the teak.

Sailing performance was also of primary concern to the owner, who had logged many miles on previous boats. To that end, the latest technology in computer models and tank testing assured the exact ratios of lift and drag and shifts in the center of lateral resistance. The testing took place at Aerohydro,

an American company based in Southwest Harbor, Maine. Of course, some could argue that this state-of-the-art aluminum hull with winglet keel and hydraulic winches could not be considered a classic, but where design aesthetics are concerned, *Alejandra* is almost without equal.

There is a large recessed center cockpit between the deckhouse and the main mast. It is obvious that this luxurious dining area had to dictate the configuration of the below deck space. Aside from the on-deck cockpit requirements of

Alejandra *is ketch-rigged and carries 716 square meters of sail. Her masts are 50 meters high! A thoroughbred sailboat by sheer grace and elegance, her design blends traditional appeal with state-of-the-art technology.*

The master stateroom that occupies the entire width of the boat has a settee to starboard and a large double bed to port. The bed is set back with a mahogany framework flanked by spiral pillars and curtains that add a mysterious air to this room.

There are three guest cabins; one with a double bed and two with twin berths, all with en suite bathrooms.

the owner, there was also the challenge of isolating the owner's stateroom from the sound of the engine room. The cockpit was therefore placed above the engine room, well forward of the master suite. The master suite, which occupies the entire width of the boat, includes a romantic curtained alcove for the owner's bed, a built-in dresser with cabinets and bookshelves in the center, and a seating area to starboard. The Cuban mahogany used throughout is exquisite. The step-up level to the lounging and bed area provide a more intimate feeling as well as a welcome visual enhancement. A large, curved alcove holds a ship's model. The arches are replicated over and over with the bookshelves and the cupboards. The overhead is a pleasant balance of mahogany beams and white painted paneling. Twisted pillars and pilasters lend a regal air.

The three guest cabins, two to starboard and one to port, are all commodious with en suite bathrooms. Like so many contemporary spaces, the din-

ing area is open to the main saloon.

The main saloon, accessed through sliding doors, is breathtaking. Twin sofas sit opposite each other and frame the fireplace. The elegance and attention to detail is obvious from every corner. One would imagine being at the Harvard Club, not on a yacht. *Alejandra* is a new classic that may set the pace for classics to come in the next century.

The dining table of solid mahogany is surrounded by cupboards and drawers with custom compartments for every piece of china, glassware and cutlery.

The main saloon is subtly lit with warm light from the walls and table lamps as well as natural light from the multi-faceted oval skylight. The black marble fireplace is the focal point.

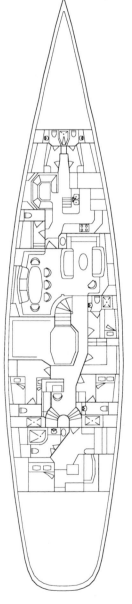

CHRISTOPHER MOORHOUSE

CHRISTOPHER MOORHOUSE

Type: Gaff Schooner
LOA: 129' 7" (39.52 m)
LOD: 107' 8" (32.80 m)
LWL: 77' 9" (23.71 m)
Beam: 20' 4" (6.2 m)
Draft: 13' 2" (4 m)
Displacement: 161 tons
Hull: Burma teak on oak frames
Designer/Builder: William Fife & Sons;
  Fairlie, Scotland.
Restoration: Southampten Yacht Services;
  Southampten, England
Year built: 1931, restored 1985–87

ALTAIR

*A*ltair was one of the last in a line of distinguished yachts designed and built by William Fife III at the Fairlie yard on the eastern bank of the Firth of the Clyde. At the age of seventy-three, Fife was delighted with the opportunity to create yet another masterpiece. Commissioned in 1929 by Captain Guy H. MacCaw, Fife's brief was "to build a sound, safe cruiser, safe to go to the South Seas Islands in with no anxiety." Fife and MacCaw had a healthy correspondence regarding the design parameters prior to the final contract. *Altair* was to be gaff rigged despite the trend of the time toward Bermudian. Furthermore, despite MacCaw's trepidations over the long overhangs (which he felt belonged exclusively on racing boats), Fife convinced him that the overhangs were an essential part of performance. The finished boat bears the unmistakable sheer and presence of a Fife. But after all the directives about how he wanted to use *Altair* for extensive cruising, MacCaw never made it beyond the French Atlantic Coast in the two years that he owned her.

MacCaw sold *Altair* to Walter Runciman, Liberal MP for St. Ives, whose father was the owner of the renowned yacht *Sunbeam*. He owned *Altair* until 1938, cruising her up the West Coast of Scotland and competing her in various Solent races. Her next owner, Sir William Verdon-Smith, sailed her for just a couple of years; then, along with many other yachts of her era, she was acquired by the Admiralty and enlisted in the war effort. After the war, in 1948, she was purchased by a Portuguese gentleman who kept her for two years. Next, Miguel Sans Mora from Barcelona discovered her and maintained a devoted relationship with her for thirty-four years! Under Mora's ownership, *Altair* had a major refit in Southampton. In 1985 she was sold to a company called Blue Wave, which decided to totally rebuild her and return her to her original glory. She was taken to

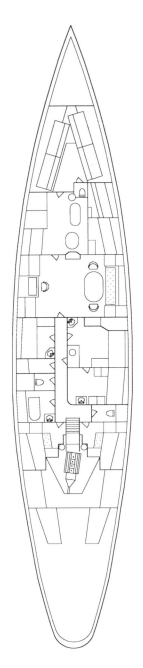

Southampton Yacht Services on the River Itchen, the successor to the Camper & Nicholsons yard that had done excellent work on *Shamrock V* and *Puritan*. She was lifted out of the water into a custom-built cradle, and a shed was constructed over her so that work could begin.

Paul Goss, skipper and project manager, oversaw the rebuilding. She was dismantled piece by piece—deckhouse, hatches, literally everything was removed down to the bare hull, and every piece was labeled and saved. All that was possible to restore, including the furniture, walnut paneling from the saloon, and so on, was removed for refurbishment. Once she was opened up, complete replacement of electrical systems and plumbing was made easier. Scotsman, Iain McAllister has provided an invaluable service to anyone interested in Fifes by painstakingly cataloguing all of Fife's original paperwork. Therefore, at the outset of *Altair*'s restoration there was a meticulous paper trail that included everything from the bill for crew uniforms to correspondence with Fife himself and the sailmaker.

Altair truly set the standard for all subsequent classic yacht restorations. The 2¼-inch Burma teak planking on oak frames was in fine condition; however, the corroded iron floors had to be replaced, and new timber had to be scarfed into the frames where it had deteriorated around metalwork. While new plumbing and wiring were fitted, the original water and fuel tanks were found to be safe and usable. A new Gardner 200 hp six-cylinder diesel was installed. Conveniences such as the water maker, washing machines, and freezers were hidden under the galley sole on a mezzanine. While some concessions bowed to modernity, every effort was made to maintain the masterpiece that Fife had created originally. When it came time to make new sails, the owner wanted Egyptian cotton; Paul Goss

thought that synthetic would be much more practical, however, so together they prevailed upon Ratsey & Lapthorn to create specially pigmented cream-colored Terylene sails. Once *Altair* paved the way, other classic yachts could also order sails to match their heritage. The interior accommodation layout remains the same: three guest cabins and his-and-hers interconnecting owner's cabins. Carpets, fabrics, and paint were researched and reproduced. The eggshell finish on the overhead cannot be distinguished from the original.

Belowdecks the decor is simple and elegant. Sitting in the main saloon, surrounded by original paneling, cabinetry, and furniture, you can truly imagine the presence of all those who sat there before you over the last sixty-six years.

Altair is one of the "queens" of the classic yacht fleet. She is expertly skippered by Steve Hammond who takes pride in every aspect of maintaining dignity in seamanship. Hammond came in late on the restoration team; in 1986–87, he and another crew member were responsible for the rigging. Hammond is passionate about his charge. He says that *Altair* is the most impeccably restored yacht of all. He credits Albert Obrist (now owner of Fairlie Restorations) for his single-minded pursuit of excellence and attention to detail. He also attributes *Altair*'s continuing upkeep to the current owner, a Spanish gentleman, who is in love with his yacht. Yachts such as *Altair* absolutely require dedicated owners and crew.

In the 1985 refit, forty percent of the 8x6-inch oak timbers were found to have wasted away. This necessitated the tricky job of scarfing in new grown frames.

The deckhouse and hatches were removed prior to complete stripping of the old yellow pine deck. The new deck is a plywood/teak composite. Although modern methodology was applied, her traditional appearance has not been altered.

Many of the deck fittings, including the winches, were recast in bronze.

The color and pattern of carpets, fabrics, and curtains were carefully researched and reproduced.

Belowdecks, all the furniture and paneling were removed for refurbishment, allowing for the replacement of plumbing and electrical systems. The walnut paneling in the main saloon and the appointments in the magnificent staterooms have been restored exactly as they were originally designed.

Altair's Oregon pine and spruce spars received a lot of attention; the main boom and bowsprit were extended back to the original length. All standing and running rigging was redesigned and replaced.

The deckhouse is light, spacious, and cozy with two settees large enough to lay down on.

Type: Yawl
LOA: 70' 5" (21.5 m)
LOD: 61' (18.60 m)
Beam: 13' 5" (4.12 m)
Draft: 9' 2" (2.80 m)
Displacement: 48 tons
Hull: Teak on white oak
Designer: Claude Worth
Builder: Philip & Sons; Dartmouth, England
Year built: 1924, refit 1982, 1990–91
Engine: Perkins 120 hp

ALZAVOLA

*A*lzavola, with her black hull and proud plum bow, is truly impressive as she cuts through the water. Designed by Claude Worth and built by Philip & Sons in 1924 in Dartmouth, England, for Sir Walter Ramsey Kay, she was originally called *Gracie III* and was a sister ship to *Tern IV*. The two yachts were actually built in tandem from the same drawings. *Gracie III*'s construction was of the best quality Rangoon teak planks on white oak double frames, fastened with copper rivets and silicon-bronze screws. Though close sisters, the two yachts were not exactly twins. *Tern* was a classic gaff cutter with a short mizzenmast, a flush deck, and small deckhouse. *Gracie*'s raised cabin and doghouse afforded more comfortable and light interior space. Also, she was significantly different in that she was rigged as a Bermudian yawl, thus easier to handle and faster when close-hauled. In 1926 she was transformed into a ketch to allow for a shorter boom and more handy mainsail. Her rig remained in that configuration until 1951, when her bowsprit was shortened at the Berthon Boat Company.

Under British flag and ownership for many years, in 1961 she was purchased by Oscar Alfred Pio, who sailed her through the Azores and around Madeira enroute to the Mediterranean. Pio, who lived in Florence with his wife and six sons, kept *Gracie III* for three years. On December 11, 1964, she was pur-

chased by the father of the current owner. Signor Zaccagni fell in love with *Gracie* at first sight. She became an important part of the family and was renamed in an effort to make her truly belong. Although many feel that renaming a boat is bad luck, the Zaccagni family felt *Alzavola*, which means teal, held more meaning than *Gracie*. Teal coincidentally has more relationship to *Tern*, but at the time of purchase, the Zaccagnis were unaware of the connection between the two yachts. All five children in the family grew up sailing on *Alzavola*. Even

Nicole and Enrico Zaccagni enjoy racing their beloved Alzavola with a crew of good friends at the Antigua Classic Yacht Regatta.

with two permanent crew members, the children participated in varnishing, polishing, and day-to-day maintenance—or as least as much as their school schedules would allow. Weekends were busy with club races; other times of the year and during holidays there were always a variety of national and international regattas. *Alzavola* would race under RORC and then IOR rules against even modern racers. During the summer months when the winds were lighter, the family enjoyed bringing out the spinnakers, drifter, and light genoas. They prided themselves on using the engine as seldom as possible.

Alzavola remained competitive despite her age and weight. She won several winter races along the west coast of Italy between 1968 and 1975. One of her more notable results was first in class in the 1971 Middle Sea Race, a tough winter race that started and ended in Malta and went around Sicily. In the years that followed, *Alzavola* proved that she could handle herself in heavy winds and heavy seas.

She was built to sail comfortably and fast. In 1979, the first year that she crossed the Atlantic to the Caribbean, she made the passage between Tenerife and St. Lucia in fourteen days under twin genoa stay sails, establishing the record for that year. Enrico

"Kiko" Zaccagni had taken over *Alzavola* from his father by now and worked her as a charter boat in the Caribbean for three years. In 1982 *Alzavola* returned to Italy for a major refit at the Esaom yard in Elba. The boat was stripped to bare wood, recaulked completely, and new electric wiring, pumps, hoses, and stainless-steel water and fuel tanks were installed. The engine and generator were overhauled, bilges and all structures were checked and painted, the masts were pulled off, checked and revarnished, and all standing rigging was replaced.

In 1982 the first annual vintage yacht race in Porto Cervo was held. *Alzavola* was certainly among the most admired. In 1983 at the same event, *Alzavola* had the distinction of beating 12-Meter *Tomahawk* first in real and elapsed time and ultimately winning third overall in a week characterized by calm or variable winds. From 1984 until 1991 she raced in many classic events, always coming away with one of the top three honors.

In 1986 Enrico officially purchased *Alzavola* from his father and to this day lives aboard with his wife, Nicole, cruising and chartering. The repairs and refits have been diligent: a new stem in Viareggio in 1990, new sails in 1991, the planking refastened, keel bolt replaced, attention paid to hull, topsides, and all rigging and hardware. As all classic yacht owners know, the process is endless.

In 1993 *Alzavola* won the vintage class at the Antigua Classic Yacht Regatta and the Stormy Weather Trophy. In 1996 at the same regatta she won again. She spends her time now in the Caribbean, between the islands and often in Venezuela. Enrico and Nicole have kept her spirit alive; they live aboard, they entertain, they sail her, they travel, and they race her. *Alzavola* thrives on the constant attention and use. *Alzavola* is perhaps the best example of a classic yacht being used as a liveaboard, but still she races and enjoys being in all the classic yacht events.

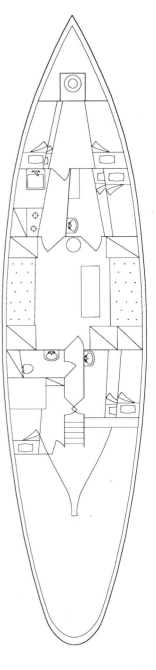

A Beken of Cowes photograph taken in the 1920s hangs on the bulkhead.

The plants, shell collections, artifacts and other personal touches truly indicate that Alzavola is a liveaboard boat.

Type: Cutter
LOA: 50' (15.24 m)
LOD: 45' 6" (13.87 m)
LWL: 36' (10.97 m)
Displacement: 39,500 lbs.
Hull: Teak on oak
Designer: Starling Burgess
Builder: Eastern Shipbuilding;
  Shelburne, Nova Scotia
Rebuilt: Rockport Marine; Rockport, Maine
Year built: 1931; rebuilt 1994
Engine: 71 hp Westerbeke Diesel

ARAWAK

rawak, under a different name, was designed by W. Starling Burgess in 1929. Burgess was much in demand in those days; the following year he was involved in the design of three winning J Boats: *Enterprise, Rainbow* and *Ranger.* There are very few of Burgess's boats left, two of the most notable ones being *Niña* and *Chips.* The original owner of *Arawak* went bankrupt in the Depression and was unable to finish the boat. John Barry Ryan from Marblehead, Massachusetts, picked up the project and continued building the boat at the Eastern Shipbuilding Company in Nova Scotia. She was finished in 1931 in Shelburne, Nova Scotia, her hull planked in 1¼-inch teak. Ryan kept telling his family that "Christmas" was coming in August. His family thought he was a silly old man. When he sailed the boat into Marblehead Neck that summer, it was obvious that *Christmas* had indeed arrived! She stayed in the Ryan family for three generations.

By the late '70s, the Ryans were having some financial difficulties, and *Christmas* was laid up at Brownell's Yard in Mattapoisett, Massachusetts, deteriorating from lack of attention. In 1980 Philip LaFrance found her in the yard and was in part able to purchase her by paying off the yard bills.

LaFrance rebuilt the boat at two different times. He sailed her proudly around New England and the Caribbean and at one time entered her in the Bermuda Race. He and his wife, Valerie, who works for *Wooden Boat* magazine were dedicated caregivers to *Christmas* for almost fifteen years.

Classic yachts require devoted patrons. Donald Tofias, a businessman from Massachusetts and an avid sailor, made a passionate snap decision to purchase *Christmas* from the LaFrances in 1994 at the Eggemoggin Reach Race in Maine. After his first sail, accompanied by two Maine wooden-boat aficionados—Taylor Allen of Rockport

Marine, and Brooklin boat builder Joel White—Tofias was encouraged to carry out a major refit. In fact, the boat was virtually rebuilt. Among the myriad changes, including painting her trademark black hull white, was a name change. *Christmas* is now *Arawak*.

Twenty-three men worked on the boat; everyone wanted to be a part of the project. She was given a new backbone, new planking, new floors, and her deck was refastened and recaulked. She was fitted with electronics, refrigeration, and new engine. The entire stern post was replaced. With the old wooden keel and new rudder, the boat was really tender, so a decision was made to design a new keel, which is now elliptical. There was more rebuilding than Tofias or the yard had originally anticipated, which added about a thousand pounds. The original mast was solid spruce, weighing over 1,200 pounds. To make the boat lighter, Eric Hall of Hall Spars in Bristol, Rhode Island, created a cream-colored mast of carbon fiber and added 8 to 10 feet to the top of the mast. Tim Wodehouse made the sails, adding 20 percent to the sail area. A new Edison quadrant pedestal steering wheel was installed, and the main boom and staysail boom were made of aluminum. Tofias was involved in all decisions.

Arawak's navigation station is small, but totally functional and secure.

Arawak competes in the various series of classic yacht regattas in New England and the Caribbean. In his refit of Arawak, Tofias chose to change her rig and use carbon fiber.

Tofias has been criticized for ruining a "perfectly good classic yacht" by imposing modern materials. He is quite candid about the controversy surrounding her refit. For instance, he chose Lewmar winches rather than trying to find bronze, because he had a bad experience with the Concordia that he owned prior to

Arawak's *accommodation is compact, elegant and thoughtfully executed. The main saloon with dining area to port and settee to starboard is classic, and the subtle taupe upholstery sets off the beautiful woodwork.*

buying *Arawak*. He had done a refit on her and found, "You can't get good bronze winches today—my bronze winches had to be constantly polished because Barient put iron filings in the bronze—the bronze winch is the chrome winch without the chrome, and the only way to hold chrome on bronze is to put iron in it." Tofias says that the Lewmar winches saved a lot of weight on *Arawak*.

Tofias is resolved about his decisions. As a founding member of the International Yacht Restoration School in Newport, Rhode Island, he feels that restoration and the teaching of it are very important. He says that the 1885 yacht *Coronet*, which is currently a project at IRYS, will and should be restored absolutely faithfully since it is being used as a learning tool. Still, he says, "I feel that if Herreshoff, Burgess, Rhodes, and the rest of them had had modern materials, they would have used them; they wouldn't have thought about it for a minute. Herreshoff, even in his glory at the height of the '20s, was building composite hulls

with bronze strapping and ultralight wood. The first dura-aluminum mast was made in the '30s, and sailmakers were experimenting with what became Dacron and nylon at that time. We've gone from iron fastening to stainless and Monel and other modern materials. Boats were at one time designed to be raced and sailed and last only fifteen to twenty years. Today we have all the modern materials; we absolutely have to use them if we choose to."

Tofias says his decisions didn't cause him anguish. "I sold much of my old stuff, so it got reused. I gave away the old mast and sails to the Maine Maritime Academy for a boat they were rebuilding." He feels that *Arawak* has the concept, spirit, and memory of the old boat. Tofias is baffled as to why the purists don't use traditional cotton sails. He loves his boat and enjoys campaigning her in all the classic yacht events from Antigua to New England. A supporter of the New England Wooden Boat series, Tofias "did it his way."

Type: Cutter
LOA: 59' 6" (18.1 m)
LWL: 40' (12.2 m)
Beam: 11' 6" (3.5 m)
Draft: 8' 6" (2.6 m)
Displacement: 26,460 lbs. (12,000 k)
Designer: Charles Nicholson
Builder: Camper & Nicholsons;
   Gosport, England
Restoration: Harry Spencer and Clark Poston
Year built: 1896; restored 1994

AVEL

vel has the distinction of being over one hundred years old! Thanks to time, talent, and (of course) money, the 60-foot cutter has had a noble rebirth.

During Victorian times, yachting was a relatively fledgling sport, and for the most part many more yachts were built in the U.K. than on the Continent. In 1896 *Avel*, which is the Breton word for wind, was the second of three yachts (of the same name) built by Charles Nicholson for Frenchman René Calame. At that time, according to yacht historian William Collier, there were only 481 French-built yachts over 10 tons and 642 French-owned yachts in existence, while in England there were 4,343 comparably sized yachts built and 3,884 plying the waters. The U.K. was unquestionably the leader in the yachting industry. It was not unusual for French owners to build and maintain their yachts in the U.K., for a number of reasons (including tax implications). Builder Charles Nicholson was quite fluent in French, which enhanced his ability to procure numerous commissions from French clients for the Camper & Nicholsons yard.

Avel was not built as a racing boat. According to an article in *Le Yacht* magazine from 1898, "She was principally built for relatively long voyages and to give her owner maximum comfort in all reasonable wind conditions." Calame raced *Avel* in a twenty-nine mile race organized by Sport Nautique de l'Ouest in St. Nazaire and came in fifth. There is no other evidence that she raced during those few years.

In 1898 *Avel* was sold to Englishman E. W. Balne, who brought her back to England and reregistered her there. In 1899 another Englishman, Arthur Carleton Nicholson, distiller of gin and veteran of the Boer War, acquired her and kept her on the East Coast at Brightlingsea for several years. He sold her in 1915. She seemed to have changed hands frequently and ulti-

A contemporary Twyfords hand basin was installed to match the original 1895 Twyfords porcelain-lined cast metal toilet bowl.

mately was purchased by Mr. Butcher of Maldon, Essex. He apparently bought her to renovate but for some reason, sold her to W. W. Cocks without realizing his plans. Unfortunately, she ended up on a mud berth at West Mersea. Her lead keel was removed because in those days the lead was worth more than the boat. Sadly, a gracious, lovely sailing boat was turned into a houseboat. In 1927 she was deleted from the British Registry of Shipping. She stayed where she was, remaining virtually unchanged; the rig was removed and a large, ugly deckhouse was added. Bought, sold, and passed on to new generations, *Avel* languished unappreciated until William Collier, who was running the vintage yacht division of Camper & Nicholsons in Cannes, discovered her and recognized her potential.

Collier brought *Avel* to the attention of John Bardon, skipper of Maurizio Gucci's three-masted schooner *Creole*. Gucci had been to the classic yacht event at the Nioulargue in St. Tropez with *Creole*, loved the spirit surrounding the classic yacht fleet, and was enticed by the idea of restoring a small vintage yacht to be used for racing. In October 1990, *Creole*'s chief officer, Niall Robinson, and sparmaker Harry Spencer of Cowes were dispatched to investigate the possibilities of *Avel*. When Spencer sketched out a rough of what *Avel* would actually look like under sail, the decision was solidified to buy her. Her purchase price was £15,000.

She was transported to Spencer's yard in Cowes, a shed was built, and her restoration began in earnest. A complete record of her measurements and detailed drawings of her interior were made. The boat was dismantled, and the experts began their work. The ultimate goal was to restore her, not just reconstruct her. Only 30 percent of the framing and a few planks had to be replaced. All that was salvageable was salvaged. The builders were very impressed by the state of the wood. The only rot was in the two ends where fresh water came in through the deck and ventilation was poor. Still, everything on deck had to be replaced. Boatbuilder Clark Posten admits that he would rather build a new boat than restore an old one. Restoring *Avel* was obviously labor intensive and time consuming. Since there were no contemporary pictures of her sail plan, Harry Spencer created a sail plan using his philosophy of "feel." Much had to be fabricated: rudder blade, stock, skeg, and, of course, spars and all the rigging right down to mast hoops

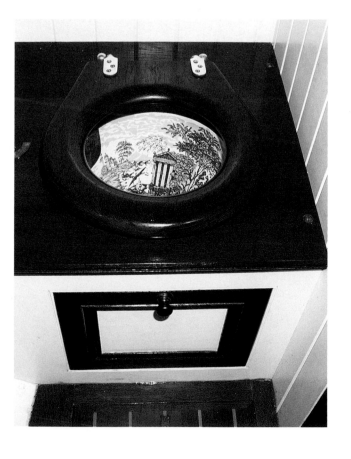

and blocks. Sails were made by Ratsey & Lapthorn out of polyester to look like traditional cotton. Hand roping and hand-worked holes, leather work, and pointing on the ropes all give *Avel* the "look" of a vintage vessel. The interior, originally built in teak with pitch pine paneling, was remarkably intact. The aft cabin has been slightly altered. The cabin sole had to be renewed throughout. According to William Collier's report on *Avel*, when the interior was reinstated, there was never more than one centimeter discrepancy between interior and restored hull. Obviously with a boat that is a hundred years old, there are places that seem worn; still, unless structure commanded change, the stressed wood was left so as not to hide the passage of time. The head became almost an obsession; the toilet—a Blundell Brothers special with a cast-metal bowl and a blue patterned porcelain lining that had TWYFORDS 1895 written on the back—was fully restored, and a contemporary Twyfords hand basin to match was installed.

Avel sails incredibly well to windward. She is sailed the old-fashioned way in that she does not have an engine and has to be towed out of tight harbors. As a tribute to Maurizio Gucci, who had a tragic and untimely death in 1995, *Avel* was brought to the Nioulargue race that he loved so much and was raced in his honor.

Avel's restoration was thorough and complete. Amazingly, when the interior was reinstalled, there was never more than one centimeter discrepancy between the interior and the restored hull. The interior is teak and pitch pine. The pine was selected for the quality of the grain pattern. The cabin sole was renewed throughout. Avel *is one hundred years old, and every attempt was made to maintain all that was original.*

Type: Yawl
LOA: 74' 3" (22.63 m)
LWL: 51' (15.54 m)
Beam: 15' 1" (4.58 m)
Draft: 9' 6"(2.74 m)
Displacement: Approximately 100,000 lbs.
Hull: Cedar and mahogany over white oak
Designer: Olin Stephens
Builder: Henry S. Nevins; City Island,
  New York
Year built: 1949; restored 1995
Engine: Perkins Diesel

B O L E R O

olero is one of those classic yachts whose very name lifts eyebrows among yacht-racing aficionados. For fifty years she has been considered one of the world's best known and prettiest ocean racers. Built for speed, she has an outstanding track record, finishing first in the 1950, 1954, and 1956 Bermuda races. Her elapsed time record for the '56 event was held for eighteen years!

Olin Stephens drew the plans for *Bolero* in 1947 for his discerning client John Nicholas Brown, then undersecretary of the United States Navy and vice-commodore of the New York Yacht Club. With a displacement of 100,000 pounds, powerful bow sections, and a relatively narrow beam of 15 feet, *Bolero* was a superb sea boat. She was built by Henry S. Nevins at his boatyard in City Island, New York. Nevins had always enjoyed the reputation of building high quality "gold platers," most of which he built in the '20s and '30s. During World War II he turned his talents to mine sweepers and fast rescue craft. After the war, it became difficult for Nevins to compete with European yards, which managed to build yachts a lot less expensively than those in the States. When Nevins launched *Bolero* on June 10, 1949, he told his wife that he thought this would be his last launching. He died the following year at the age of seventy-two.

Only the best materials were put into *Bolero*. Double-planked cedar and mahogany were carefully

laid over white oak frames. Monel strapping along the inside of the hull and around the chainplates and mast step added additional strength to the structure. Port Orford cedar was used instead of teak to lighten the hull by 1,500 pounds. The two masts were state-of-the-art aluminum. (No one would deny that *Bolero* was a classic, yet she was never conceived with wooden spars.) Commodore Brown loved his boat and sailed

Good visibility, convient navigation area, a roomy pilot berth and protection from the elements make the dog-house a well-used area.

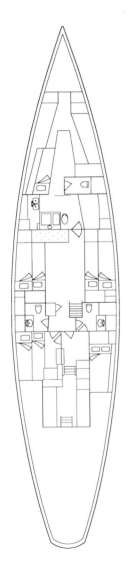

her hard. A roster of pedigreed sailors such as "Corny" Shields—famous tactician and helmsman—Olin and Rod Stephens, and "Doc" Davidson of the Stevens Institute model-testing tank were often invited to sail on her.

Brown sold *Bolero* to Swedish businessman Sven Salen in 1955. She remained mostly in Europe except for a time in the early '60s when she was owned by Bob Keefe, commodore of San Francisco's St. Francis Yacht Club. When the current owner, Gunter Sunkler, found her in 1989, she was in very sorry condition, languishing in the weeds in a canal in Ft. Lauderdale. Sunkler had been tracking *Bolero* for years and was determined to resurrect her. An Austrian-born restaurateur from the Chesapeake, Sunkler enlisted the services of Alan Gilbert, chief engineer at Sparkman & Stephens, to decide how to go about her restoration. Gilbert was delighted to be involved with one of S & S's pet boats. Of the project he said, "I am old enough to know what wood is, and I have learned over the years that restoration, especially one that involves wood, requires a burning passion and a complete commitment to the project." *Bolero* was fortunate to have found a dedicated owner.

She had been stripped of every piece of gear for her owner's nonpayment of services. It took Sunkler three years to locate and buy back masts, booms, sails, and whatever else he could find that had belonged to her. Sunkler changed yards three times before settling for the right one to restore his beloved *Bolero*. He wanted to restore the boat to her original condition as much as possible; however, he did modify the rig and sail plan to be able to sail her with just his family instead of a full racing crew. Also, high strength fiberglass sections were sistered in alongside the oak

frames to add strength where electrolysis had set in next to the fuel tanks. Belowdecks, moisture damage necessitated a careful reconstruction of interior paneling. The bulkheads were repainted the original white, and the settees were reupholstered in a rich tufted red leather. The towels, china, and glassware were replaced using the original patterns, and every latch and hinge were removed and rechromed. Restoration for Sunkler, as with so many classic yacht owners, had become an obsession. Even the date of the recommissioning was the anniversary of the launching, forty-seven years later. Sunkler took great pleasure sending the exact same invitations to the event that had been sent out by John Nicholas Brown—with only the time and place being changed.

Moisture damage necessitated a careful reconstruction of interior paneling. The bulkheads were repainted the original white, and the settees were reupholstered in rich tufted red leather. The overall feeling below is formal, clean, and elegant.

Type: Schooner
LOA: 144' 2" (43.95 m)
LOD: 131' 2" (40 m)
LWL: 98' 5" (30 m)
Beam: 28' 6" (8.67 m)
Draft: 13' 1" (4 m)
Displacement: 225 tons
Hull: Aluminum
Designer: Lunstroo Custom Design; Holland
Interior Designer: John Munford
Builder: Royal Huisman Shipyard; Holland
Year built: 1994
Engine: 1 x 650 hp MTU 12V 183TE62 diesel

BORKUMRIFF III

Borkumriff III was conceived as a true modern classic by her German owners and their Dutch naval architect, Hank Lunstroo. The inspiration for her design came from *Bluenose*, the famous 130-foot Nova Scotia schooner built in 1921. The owners' former yacht, *Borkumriff II*, also a Lunstroo design, provided the motivation for them to build a new boat incorporating all of their experience and ideas. To that end, in addition to Lunstroo they chose Henk Wimmers, a former design director for the Dutch Navy, as project manager, the Royal Huisman Shipyard as builder, and John Munford as interior designer. The "classic" approach to the hull shape was of paramount importance at the outset. Similar to *Bluenose, Borkumriff III* is also a massive boat with a long keel, which enables her to sail well in a heavy sea. Built of modern materials—aluminum with aluminum spars—she has a traditional profile: a fine, long clipper bow, a slightly overhung stern, and a lovely wineglass transom. Her open bulwarks topped with a varnished cap rail and stanchions rising to 24 inches above her teak-planked decks add to the old-fashioned look. Also, her sails—computer designed by Hood—were built of Dacron in a narrow paneled design and dyed an Egyptian-cot-

ROY OWEN ROBERTS

ton cream color, and the clew and tack rings were hand finished with leather.

Her classic schooner aesthetics are combined with a panoply of modern technical systems. Forty-one winches, 23 of them hydraulic, enable *Borkumriff III* to be handled easily with minimum crew. The traffic and command center is the teak-paneled deckhouse with a trio of windows on each side and an opening skylight. Here there is a dinette with bench seating upholstered in blue leather, and a settee opposite that doubles as a watch berth. From the deckhouse, the compan-

ionway leads both forward to the main saloon and aft to the owner's stateroom. John Munford has succeeded once again in creating the "gentleman's club" look. The owners had chosen Munford primarily because of his work on *Endeavour*. As with Elizabeth Meyer's world-famous J Boat, the joinery is exemplary.

The saloon is open the full width of the 28-foot 6-inch beam. To starboard is an intimate dining area for six, featuring a circular cherry coffee table that functions as a display case for an antique gimbaled compass recessed in its center. On the bulkhead, flanked by twin bookcases are half models depicting the former Borkumriffs. Decorative raised-paneled cabinetry conceals entertainment electronics, bar, and the base of the main mast. To port is the formal dining/lounge area with elegant button-backed leather upholstery. Aft are the stately owner's study, stateroom, and bath. Twin beds are divided by a sofa and breakfast table. Forward of the saloon are mirror-image guest staterooms, each with ensuite showers.

Every detail of *Borkumriff III*—from her engine room to her deck plan and throughout her interior accommodation—has been extremely well thought out. All available space has been used for some functional purpose. Craftsmanship and joinery work are of the superb quality one has come to associate with Royal Huisman Shipyard. *Borkumriff III* is a modern classic, the result of teamwork and owners who were often on site and knew what they wanted.

Aft are the stately owner's study, stateroom, and bath. Twin beds are divided by a sofa and breakfast table.

There are two identical guests cabins port and starboard which are painted white and trimmed in cherry.

BILL MUNCKE

KO WELLMAN

The main saloon features a circular cherry table that also functions as a display case for an antique gimbaled compass recessed in its center.

The deckhouse provides an additional dining area with a trio of windows on each side and a large opening skylight. The navigation center and a settee that doubles as a watch berth is also housed here.

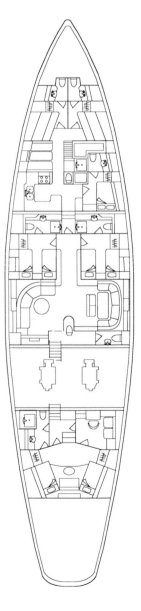

Type: Motor Yacht
LOA: 111' (33.8 m)
LWL: 104' 4" (31.8 m)
Beam: 18' 6" (5.6 m)
Draft: 7' 5" (2.7 m)
Displacement: 280 tons
Hull: Teak on oak
Builder: A. M. Dickie & Sons; Bangor, Wales
Year built: 1930; restored 1994
Engines: 2 x 240 Mercedes diesels

CLASSIQUE

lassique was built for Mr. W. G. Hetherington in Wales in 1930 and launched with the name *Janetha IV*. At 111 feet, she was the largest wooden boat that A. M. Dickie & Sons ever built. Her hull is teak on oak frames, the bottom is coppered, and the planking, decks, and deckhouse are also teak. Her interior paneling is Honduran mahogany. In the main saloon and some of the staterooms, the finish is highly polished; in others, there is an ivory enamel finish.

Until the Second World War, *Janetha IV* sailed primarily in Scottish waters. However, she made at least one Atlantic crossing to the United States. Once in the States, she is purported to have entertained President Roosevelt on numerous occasions. Back in the U.K., she was requisitioned by the British Royal Navy in 1939 and run as a patrol boat under the name HMS *Gomax*. She even participated in the retrieval of troops from Dunkirk across the channel to Britain. Faint bullet holes made by aircraft during her rescue missions still visible on her decks attest to her war effort.

From 1950–1953 *Classique* spent time around the Italian and French Rivieras and then was sold to a Greek tycoon. Under the name *Ismini III*, she sailed out of Piraeus as a private yacht until 1988, at

which time she was purchased by the Craig family. That year *Classique* played a minor role in the movie *Pascoli's Island*, starring Helen Mirren and Ben Kingsley. Because of her vintage and appearance, she was well cast in this period film.

In 1993, Claus and Birgit Santon watched *Classique* motor into the old port of Nice and were immediately attracted to her. Santon is a Danish naval architect and shipbuilder, living in the south of France. He originally saw *Classique* in Greece some twenty-five years before and had fallen in love with her at that time. In 1994 the Santons purchased her, and *Classique* became a family enterprise.

Claus and Birgit Santon and their children, Christopher and Christine, all participated in lovingly restoring her. Completely renovated, she still maintains all of her original charm. *Classique* is now used for charter, and due to her special nature she has been used in the advertising campaigns for the likes of Martini and Louis Vuitton as well as for private charters for a variety of illustrious personalities on the Côte d'Azur. In 1994 she won second prize for elegance at the Monaco Classic Week and third prize overall. In 1996 *Classique* received first prize for motor yachts.

EDWARD HOLT

EDWARD HOLT

Classique's *Edwardian heritage is visible
everywhere—on deck and below. The
saloon and staterooms are lined with rich
panels of Honduran mahogany, some
highly polished, others have an ivory
enamel finish.*

Type: Schooner
LOA: 214' 3" (65.30 m)
LOD: 191' (58.22 m)
LWL: 140' (42.67 m)
Beam: 31' (9.44 m)
Draft: 17' 6" (5.35 m)
Displacement: 525 tons
Hull: Teak
Designer: Charles Nicholson
Builder: Camper & Nicholsons; England
Year built: 1927; rebuilt 1984–86
Engine: 2 x 890 hp MTU

CREOLE

*C*reole, under the ownership of the late Maurizio Gucci, finally realized her full potential as the world's most extraordinary yacht. This 214-foot (65m) three-masted schooner was designed by Charles E. Nicholson and built by Camper & Nicholsons in 1927 for American Alexander Smith Cochran. Launched as *Vira*, she was the largest yacht that C & N had ever constructed. Nicholson went to great lengths to design a rig that could be handled with minimum crew; no spars had to be hoisted aloft, and all sails were self-tacking. Cochran was experienced with large yachts as he had been involved with *Shamrock IV* in the 1920 America's Cup and had been owner of *Westward*, *Vanitie*, and *Warrior*, so Nicholson was shocked and dismayed when Cochran insisted on cutting down the rig, ten feet from the top and ten feet from the bottom. Nicholson had advised him to balance out the boat by removing a portion of the 90-ton keel, to no avail. After a tumultuous trip to Mallorca, Cochran cabled Nicholson to complain and ended up having the lead keel removed, lead ballast stowed inside, and a false keel put back on. This was not what Nicholson had intended!

Vira was bought by Major Maurice Pope of the Royal Yacht Squadron in 1928, whereupon he changed her name to *Creole* and lengthened her fore and main masts by ten feet. He used her as a day motor sailer in the Solent and as a ferry to Cowes. For some inexplicable reason her beautiful interior veneers of mahogany, cedar, and sycamore were painted over. In 1937 she was purchased by Sir Connop Guthrie, who decided to put *Creole* right again. The lead keel was replaced, draft was added on, as was additional length to the three masts. During the Second World War, the British Admiralty requisitioned her, renamed her *Magic Circle*, and stripped out her interior. After the war she was returned without her masts.

73

The raised helm station forward of the main deck saloon allows the skipper, John Bardon, all-around visibility. Because of her size, sailing Creole *is more like running a ship than a yacht.*

Since Guthrie had died, Camper & Nicholsons took the opportunity to purchase her. The yard sold her to Greek shipping magnate Stavros Niarchos in 1948. Niarchos was at last an owner who was ostensibly worthy of *Creole*. At the outset, he had a lot of work to do on her. Her main saloon was hung with incredible works of art by Salvador Dali, Van Gogh, Renoir Picasso, and Cezanne. Niarchos took pride in refurbishing her so that he could entertain aboard. Unfortunately, he became widowed and lost interest in *Creole*. Deteriorating in Piraeus Harbor for a time, she was purchased by a group of Danish schoolteachers as a training vessel for the Tall Ships. During this time she was worked fairly hard without the resources to keep her up.

Creole requires a lot of time and money—it was extremely fortunate that Maurizio Gucci took a fancy to *Creole* and purchased her in 1983. He lavished attention on her and systematically rebuilt the boat to the very highest standards. Work was carried out in Italy, at Lürssen in Germany, and at Astilleros de Mallorca in Palma. Gucci's skipper, John Bardon, was very much involved in the renovation process. The hull was stripped and teak planking replaced as needed. New tanks, pipes, and wiring were installed. Spencer of Cowes took charge of rerigging the boat, and Ratsey & Lapthorn and North supplied new sails.

A dazzling new interior was fitted out between 1984 and 1986. Much thought was given to keeping her style within the time frame of her original launching.

You can enter the deck saloon through four full-height glass-paneled doors that can be folded back to open the saloon to the aft deck and seating area. The sole is mahogany and oak, and the paneling is limed oak. The white suede buttoned sofas add lightness to this imposing room. The most dramatic piece of furniture here is an Austrian mid-nineteenth century oval ebony and ivory table supported by two black unicorns entwined by sea serpents. The dining saloon can be reached from a stairway adjacent to the deck saloon. The gimbaled dining table, designed by John Munford, can be folded and lowered mechanically, and a central piece can be lifted out to create two tables. The wall paneling here is quite unusual; the lower part is bird's-eye maple and burled walnut, while the upper half is "papered" with ray skins from Japan, which gives a leathered look.

The owner's stateroom has eclectic antique furniture—an Austrian writing desk, a French screen, Russian side tables, and Tiffany lamps. The paneling is maple and mahogany. This stateroom and the four exquisite guest cabins all have oil paintings from the Middle East and the Orient done by nineteenth-century European artists. Exotica permeates every aspect of the interior.

The aesthetics of *Creole* are truly extraordinary, but sailing on her in a stiff breeze is the most extraordinary aspect of this boat. She can easily reach a speed of 17 knots under sail. Gucci was extremely proud of *Creole*—in owning her, he joined the ranks of classic yacht caretakers and owners and enjoyed participating in the classic events such as the Nioulargue. The year of Gucci's death, his devoted skipper, John Bardon, raced both *Creole* and (Gucci's) *Avel* at the Niouargue as a tribute to him. With her protector gone, *Creole*'s current fate is undecided.

CREOLE

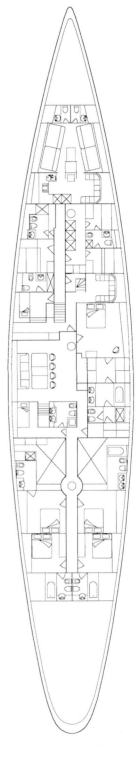

The main deck saloon is easily accessible through four folding
doors, yet there is always the pleasant option of shaded
on-deck entertaining and dining.

BUGSY GEDLEK

The imposing main saloon has limed oak paneling and white suede sofas. The sole is oak inlaid with mahogany. In front of the lounge area is an eye-catching mid-nineteenth century ebony and ivory table suppported by two black unicorns. The unicorn theme has been adopted as an emblem for Creole, *often appearing on the cutlery, crystal, and even the crew uniforms.*

Each of the four cabins has a different name and theme with corresponding decor. The guest cabin pictured here is called "the mahogany cabin."

The master stateroom is sumptuous, paneled in maple with mahogany detailing. There is warm ambient light in this room—an inviting leather armchair sits in front of a lacquered French screen that has sea shells hand-painted on glass.

Type: J Class Sloop
LOA: 129' 8" (39.56 m)
LWL: 88' 2" (26.88 m)
Beam: 22' (6.78 m)
Draft: 15' 7" (4.76 m)
Displacement: 16,565 kg
Hull: Steel
Designer: Charles Nicholson
Builder: Camper & Nicholsons; England
Rebuilt: Royal Huisman Shipyard; Holland
Year built: 1934; restored 1989
Engine: Caterpillar 3406, 259 kW (352 hp)

ENDEAVOUR

Endeavour, a 130-foot J Class sloop, was built in 1934 by Camper & Nicholsons of Gosport, England, to challenge for the America's Cup. She was commissioned by airplane magnate Sir T. O. M. Sopwith, who applied aviation technology to her rig and winches, sparing no expense to create the most powerful yacht of her day. It was the height of the J Class era and in 1934 *Endeavour* won the first two races against Vanderbilt's *Rainbow* but lost the third, deciding race. There were only ten J Class yachts built in all. They raced for the America's Cup in 1930, 1934, and 1937. Sopwith built a new *Endeavour* to compete in the 1937 cup race and sold his first yacht to Englishman Herman Andreae, who campaigned her in a series of races in Britain's Big Class before the war put an end to it all. Many of the large racing yachts were scrapped and their lead ballast was used to make bullets.

DANA JINKINS

In 1947, after having been laid up during the war, *Endeavour* was sold to Charles Kiridge. Her subsequent owners were Richard and Renée Lucas. In the '50s and '60s Big Class racing was over. In 1967 a syndicate of Americans bought *Endeavour* to restore her; however, they didn't succeed in their plan. Neither did Britain's Maritime Trust, who bought her in 1973 for the same purpose. She was sitting in the mud on the Isle of Wight when John and Vivienne Amos and Graham Jack bought her for £10. They patched up the holes in her hull with plastic bags, enabling her to float again, and moved her across the Solent to an abandoned seaplane base near Southampton.

It was at this point that Elizabeth Meyer saw *Endeavour* and fell in love with her. She says, "When I found her she just swept me off my feet. There she was, the most beautiful of all the Js, all empty inside and looking like an upside-down cathedral. Since I could buy

Endeavour, *a 130-foot J Class sloop, was built to challenge for the America's Cup. Aviation technology was used to design her rig and winches, sparing no expense to create the most powerful yacht of her day. A J Boat under sail is a breathtaking sight.* Endeavour *is one of three remaining Js in the world today.*

her, I had no choice but to do so." Meyer bought *Endeavour* from the Amoses and in 1984 began a five-year restoration. Meyer, a young American heiress and inveterate yachtswoman, is famous for tackling problems with gusto and enthusiasm. The resurrection of *Endeavour* became her mission in life. Since the hull was too fragile to move, Meyer had a building constructed over it. The steel frames and hull plating were repaired, the missing keel and ballast replaced, and a new rudder fabricated.

Once seaworthy, she was towed to Holland, put on a barge, and transported to the Royal Huisman Shipyard. There the mast, boom, and rigging were designed and built, the engine, generators and mechanical systems installed, and the interior joinery work completed. Frank Murdoch, chief engineer of the Sopwith Camel, had worked on the original *Endeavour* and at the age of 85 was on hand for most of the restoration, as well.

Her interior, designed by John Munford, is similar to the 1934 configuration, providing accommodation for eight charter guests in four staterooms—two with queen-size berths, one with a king-size bed, and one with twin berths. The staterooms adjoin bathrooms with nickel-plated shower enclosures and heated towel bars. The master bath has a large tub.

Forward of the staterooms is the saloon and dining area (22' X 14') Her raised paneling is cherry, and the cabinets have beveled glass. A beautiful working fireplace adds to the "Edwardian club" atmosphere. Her cabin soles are quarter-sawn German locust, selected to compliment the cherry. Skylights and deck prisms help illuminate the interior, avoiding the darkness of most flush-deck yachts.

Endeavour is the largest sloop in the world, carrying over 9,000 square feet of sail. In August 1989 Meyer organized the first in a series of match races in Newport, Rhode Island, between *Endeavour* and *Shamrock V*. Ted Turner and Gary Jobson were brought in as guest helmsmen, switching between *Endeavour* and *Shamrock V* for each of the three races. Though together they were an elegant sight, it was obvious that the older, lighter *Shamrock V* made of wood was not a match for the powerful steel *Endeavour*.

For the longest time, the only legacy of the J Boat era were a few photos and a handful of relics. Thanks to a few people who had a vision and a passion—and capital—there are three J Boats in existence today: *Endeavour, Shamrock V,* and *Velsheda. Velsheda* is currently undergoing a major restoration in England. Perhaps there will be an opportunity for another match race in the future!

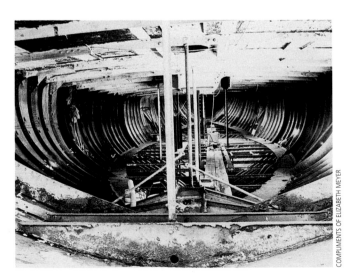

ENDEAVOUR

The completed hull against the flat backdrop of the Dutch countryside was imposing indeed!

According to owner Elizabeth Meyer, an inconceivable amount of work, love, and agony went into achieving Endeavour's present level of perfection.

Complex electronic and mechanical systems were thoroughly designed well before the interior joinery was completed.

Endeavour's *exquisite main saloon and dining area is 22' X 14' The raised cherry paneling is handsomely offset by a locust cabin sole. Despite the fact that she has a flush deck, the skylights and deck prisms create a lot of light below.*

The interior layout provides accommodation for eight charter guests in four cabins; the master stateroom has a king-size bed, and beautiful built-in cabinetry including a writing table and a bathroom with a large tub. Two of the guest cabins have queen-size berths, one has twin berths—all are commodious and comfortable.

she was in Gibraltar, her telegraph engine controls forced her forward instead of in reverse, causing major damage to the bow. She was cemented up, brought back to the Clyde, and given a major refit in 1965–66. Then, inexplicably, her name was changed back to *Henry Morgan*. From 1972–77, she was owned by John Batty, who chartered her quite successfully in the Mediterranean. In 1973–74, she underwent another refit, this time in Las Palmas. After that she apparently suffered from neglect and in 1976 was taken out of the water. In 1977 her new owner, Albert Mathews, attempted to organize a round-the-world charter. Unfortunately, despite his efforts, *Henry Morgan* remained in Palma, Mallorca, and a company purchased the boat in 1978. One of the directors of the company was Mark Cavendish, who skippered the boat across the Atlantic to Barbados. Prior to the crossing, the boat was impounded in Dakar, and one of the owners, Chuck Blue, was arrested for debts on

The main saloon is compact and cozy with polished wood paneling, rich upholstery, and thick carpeting.

The dining room, which is forward and accessed by a deck door, maintains the feel of an Edwardian club.

the boat. After clearing up these matters, the trip became even more eventful when several mechanical things went wrong—steering, refrigeration, and taking in of water. With the pumps not working, she limped into Barbados, and she was impounded yet again for various debts that the owners had incurred.

In 1981–82, a new bridge, wheelhouse and captain's quarters were built, all electronics were replaced, and the engines rebuilt. A lot of money was pumped into the boat at that time. In 1984 the refit was even more complete. In the United States at this juncture, the entire interior was stripped out and redesigned in keeping with her age of construction. She was then ready to cruise Vancouver, California, Central America, through the Panama Canal, back to the Caribbean, and then back to the Mediterranean. In 1986-87, she again underwent a refit. She is currently owned by a corporation and used for charter. Her interior has been refurbished, and she is now maintained in impeccable condition. *Henry Morgan* is a gracious, comfortable classic.

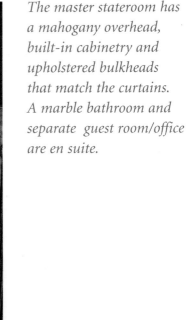

The master stateroom has a mahogany overhead, built-in cabinetry and upholstered bulkheads that match the curtains. A marble bathroom and separate guest room/office are en suite.

Type: Ketch
LOA: 125' 5" (38.25 m)
LWL: 100' (30.50 m)
Beam: 27' 8" (8.46 m)
Draft: centerboard up 9' 8" (3 m)
Draft: centerboard down 28' 5" (8.7 m)
Displacement: 190 tons
Hull: Mahogany
Designer: Bruce King Yacht Design
Interior Designer: Andrew Winch Designs
Builder: Abeking & Rasmussen;
* Lemwerder, Germany*
Year built: 1993
Engine: 12 v MTU 183 TE 92

HETAIROS

Hetairos is most definitely a new classic. Designed by Bruce King, who has a distinct penchant for traditional precepts, *Hetairos*—with her low freeboard, sweeping sheerline, and raked masts—is an exquisite example of how modern materials and engineering can work to create an aesthetic ideal. It is rare to find someone who would choose to build a wooden boat of the size of *Hetairos.* The German businessman who commissioned her had previously owned a 65-foot Henry Scheel design built in alloy at the Royal Huisman Shipyard, which he sailed for nine years before deciding to build his dream boat.

Years of research went into the final brief, and the building contract eventually went to Abeking & Rasmussen in Lemwerder, Germany. Construction began in 1991, and *Hetairos* was launched in 1993. Her hull was planked with six layers of mahogany, sheathed in fiberglass, and painted in jet-black Awlgrip with a gold cove line. The deck is teak, and the frames, stringers, and deck beams are laminated. The exterior of the deckhouse is teak, while the interior is mahogany. The curvaceous cockpit is teak with vertical surfaces varnished. The description that first came to the owner's mind—and has been repeated many times since—is that *Hetairos* is his vision of a "symphony in wood."

Hetairos is simply breathtaking—at anchor, under sail, and even stern to a dock. When you go below,

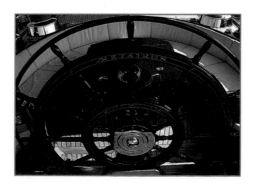

you are even more impressed. The interior is another one of Andrew Winch's masterpieces. At the foot of the companionway, on a level above the saloon, is a midstation pilothouse. The navigation station is more clublike than nautical; there is a large wooden desk and twin swiveling armchairs flanking it. On the portside is a raised table with tufted-leather settees.

Forward of the pilot house and down one level is the extraordinary main saloon. There is a vastness to the room as it

With over 7,300 square feet of sail, Hetairos is powerful under sail.

This "new classic" has carbon fiber spars painted a traditional cream color. The mainmast towers 137 feet above the deck

The curvaceous cockpit is graceful as well as functional. Curves, arches and circles create a theme that recurs in the interior as well as on deck.

spans the full beam of the boat (27' 8"). As Bruce King states in his plans, "The deck beams are the deck beams. The bottom of the deck is just that; no suspended ceilings or other covers to hide wires, plumbing, and other visual unpleasantness… Much of the structure must be visually attractive as well as be integrated with the overall aesthetic design of the total yacht." Therefore, the massive laminated beam that goes across the whole saloon is there for strength, but it just happens to be conceived with beauty. To starboard is a lovely lounge area, with a desk, a wood-burning stove, and an eccentric area—like a throne—built for the owner to sit surrounded by a curved bar from which he can dispense drinks. The large built-in birdcage has hosted a variety of tropical birds but is currently without residents. To port is a dining table inlaid with crustacea. An upholstered settee is opposite wooden chairs.

The murals that adorn the bulkheads were paint-ed by the artist David Barker and feature scenes from the Seychelles. Andrew Winch had to perform some tricky manipulations in order to achieve the end result. The panels had to be constructed, painted in a bone-colored epoxy, then shipped to the artist, who in turn painted his scenes of flora and fauna in acrylics. These murals and the friezes done by London artist Dick Young are definitely focal points in the main saloon.

The owner's stateroom and the guest cabins are all commodious with en suite bathrooms. Each one is beautifully appointed. Fine details and exquisite taste are obvious throughout the boat. A dream boat by anyone's standards, *Hetairos* was not just built to sit in port and look pretty; she was built to sail and take long voyages. The first year the owner had her, he took his family to the South Pacific and halfway around the world, including Antarctica. *Hetairos* is not old enough to be a legend, but she is off to a good start.

The interior accommodation is multi-leveled—on the first level down is a pilot house that has a large table with leather-covered settees to port and a navigation station to starboard.

The spacious well-equipped galley is forward of the main saloon. It has Corian countertops, lots of working space, and is both modern and beautiful. The configuration of the counters allows the cook to be secure under way.

The owner's stateroom is a few steps down and aft of the pilothouse. A king-size bed sits in a curtained alcove to port. A mirrored vanity flanked by bookcases is next to the bed and a writing desk and settee are to starboard. A huge skylight identical to the one in the main saloon lets in a lot of light.

Twin and double guest cabins to port and starboard accommodate up to eight guests. Each has its own head with a shared shower.

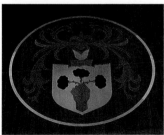

The main saloon is sweepingly grand. Well lit with a decagonal skylight, there is a dining area with a settee and wooden-backed chairs to port and a lounge area to starboard. The dining table is inlaid with crustacea. A mahogany writing desk conceals an electric piano. An eccentric bar, which is like a throne, sits to one side. The forward bulkheads contain large murals featuring scenes from the Seychelles.

Type: Yawl
LOA: 72' (21.95 m)
LWL: 55' (16.76 m)
Beam: 16' 5" (5 m)
Draft: 10' 2" (3.08 m)
Displacement: 50 tons
Hull: Mahogany on acacia
Designer: Illingworth & Primrose;
    Emsworth, England
Builder: Cantieri Naval Technica; Anzio, Italy
Year built: 1965; rebuilt 1987
Engine: GM 4-53, 140 hp

KATHLEEN

Kathleen was built in 1965 under the name *Hermitage* at the Cantieri Naval Technica in Anzio, Italy. She was designed by Renato Levi, who was the yard manager there. At the time of her launch, *Hermitage* was the largest yacht (73 feet) that Levi had ever designed. His original brief was to design a comfortable cruising boat with a simple rig, easily handled with few crew. A month or so after the keel was laid, the owner decided he wanted the boat to race in some of the more important Mediterranean events, such as the Giraglia. This meant changing the plans to an all-out racing rig. John Illingworth and Angus Primrose designed a powerful rig. During her first Giraglia race she came in second, close behind the number one boat. She continued to race with some success in Europe under the maximum handicap rating allowed by the Royal Offshore Racing Club. When racing sailors adopted the new International Offshore Rule, *Hermitage* suddenly became old-fashioned. She retired from racing and returned to the yard in Italy for some interior change: a new port cabin, new galley, and additional storage.

After several years in the Mediterranean, the spacious boat was bought by a couple who sailed her to the Caribbean. They changed her name to *Zorra* and used her for charter out of St. Thomas in the U.S. Virgin Islands, with accommodation for six to eight guests and three crew. After operating as a charter boat, her history becomes a little vague. Sometime prior to 1986 she was seized by U.S. Customs as an asset of a drug dealer. Automatically, she became a U.S. flag vessel. Docked in Norfolk, Virginia, in January 1986, she caught fire and sustained enough damage to be declared a total loss. Soon afterward, the insurance

company sold her at auction to Gannon & Benjamin of Vineyard Haven, Massachussetts. *Zorra* was fully restored at the G & B boat yard, including extensive rebuilding of her decks, deckhouse, and much of her interior and rewiring and repowering. For nearly ten years they chartered her in New England in the summer and in the Caribbean in the winter. President Clinton and his family sailed on *Zorra* during their summer holidays in Martha's Vineyard.

Jim and Kathleen Feeney bought *Zorra* in May 1996 and changed her name to *Kathleen.* They have fit her with some new sails, new interior carpentry, some new rigging, new fabrics, and also some engine work. They use her for pleasure and for some charter.

ANNE CONVERSE

ANNE CONVERSE

*There are three private guest cabins—
one with a double berth and two with
uppers and lowers.*

*The galley runs amidships in an
L-shaped configuration the full width
of the boat.*

*The navigation station is on the port
side tucked in between the galley and
main saloon.*

*Kathleen's main saloon has the classical
appeal of linen paint with mahogany
cabinetry and trim.*

Type: Schooner
LOA: 105' (32 m)
LOD: 80' (24.38 m)
LWL: 65' (19.81 m)
Beam: 19' (5.82 m)
Draft: 7' 6" (2.32 m)
Hull: Steel
Designer: Thomas Colvin
Builder: Mark Treworgy; Palm Coast, Florida
Year built: 1995
Engine: John Deere diesel

KATHRYN B.

Kathryn B., a romantic three-masted schooner, represents the culmination of a knowledgeable owner and years of yachting experience. Gordon Baxter and his wife, Kathy, conceived their latest yacht to accommodate ten guests comfortably for charter in Maine in the summers and the Caribbean in the winter. To understand where *Kathryn B.* came from, it is interesting to follow the evolution of Baxter's previous boats.

Baxter grew up in Charlottesville, Virginia, on a beautiful farm designed by Thomas Jefferson. His family's two passions were horses and sailing. At the age of six, Baxter was cruising on his parents' classic yacht in the Chesapeake, around Bermuda, and in the Bahamas. After a tour of duty with the United States Navy, Baxter went to college and bought his first classic, a 22 footer. From there he kept escalating in size. Eventually he found a derelict hull of a Dutch barge, put an engine and an interior in her, and did

a fourteen-month trip through France and Germany with her; then he had her rigged. He next ordered a 48-foot Paul Hanna yawl in Malden, England. Built of Iroko on oak frames and sporting flax sails, she was a whimsical yacht called *Moondancer*. He sold his Dutch barge to the Dutch Merchant Marine Academy to be used as a training ship for cadets and sailed *Moondancer* to Bequia in the Caribbean. There he met Kathy in 1977, sold *Moondancer*, and immediately started building his next classic, a 65-foot gaff-rigged schooner called *Memory*. She had a ten-ton cargo hold amidships, which the Baxters used to transport coffee from Venezuela to the Windward Islands and Haitian art and wooden products to the East Coast of the States.

The Baxters lived aboard *Memory* for twelve years; their daughter, Ashley, was conceived onboard in the middle of the Atlantic enroute to the Caribbean. Several years later, after their twin sons were born, the Baxters felt

This newly-launched 105-foot ocean-going three-masted, gaff-rigged topsail schooner is heavily built, but provides a graceful profile under sail.

Kathryn B.'s galley is functional and beautiful. The counter tops adjacent to the sink are copper, and the counter opposite is maple. The storage is well organized and much of it is open for easy access.

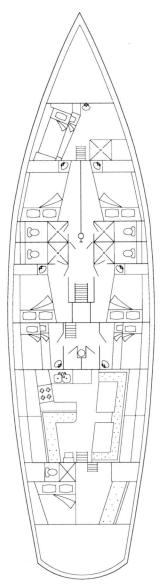

they had outgrown *Memory*, and started dreaming about the *Kathryn B.* According to Kathy Baxter, her husband has always had a love affair with boats: "He drinks them in his mind, spirit, and soul. Small boats, large boats, powerboats, sailboats—anything with classic appeal. He loves the process of designing and building a boat, perfecting every aspect."

The plans for *Kathryn B.* were for a Coast Guard-approved three-masted schooner designed by Tom Colvin. The Baxters shortened the rig by three feet so that she could go up and down the Intracoastal Waterway. They decided to have Mark Treworgy build their boat at his yard in Palm Coast, Florida, because he had a reputation for excellence in steel construction. *Kathryn B.* was christened on October 17, 1995. A makeshift interior was hastily organized, and Baxter and two friends motored her north during blizzards and bad weather, arriving in Maine in the middle of December. They hired Tom Bournival and his crew of two craftsmen to finish the interior. Many other Maine

artisans were tapped; Sheepscot River Pottery made the porcelain sinks and matching cabinet knobs that are in every cabin, Frank Luke created the brass fireplace, and a Maine craftswoman made the custom tiles—depicting the boat under sail—in the front of the fireplace. The color scheme of the interior is cream and navy. Kathy, who has been designing clothes for years, made monogrammed duvet covers for all the beds. She wanted each stateroom to feel special, so they each have oriental carpets and brass lamps and porcelain sinks. Since *Kathryn B.* was custom built for charter and not converted from another use, all her cabins are equally comfortable. The main saloon with its tufted-velvet settee is the social center at meal times. The open galley is part of the main saloon, which promotes a friendly family atmosphere.

On deck, you feel as though you are on a ship. *Kathryn B.* is sturdily built and responds well in heavy weather. She is very new, but in concept and looks she is a classic.

The main saloon and galley are open to each other, providing a family-style atmosphere for the charter guests. The dining area is to starboard and a tufted-velvet settee and fireplace are to port just aft of the galley counter.

Type: Ketch
LOA: 100' (30.48 m)
LOD: 84' (25.6 m)
LWL: 60' (18.29 m)
Beam: 17' 4" (5.28 m)
Draft: 10' 2" (3.1 m)
Displacement: 65 tons
Hull: Pine on oak
Designer/Builder: William Fife and Sons;
 Fairlie, Scotland
Restoration: Fairie Restorations; Hamble, U.K.
Year built: 1922 ; restored 1995

KENTRA

Kentra, unlike so many Fifes, was not built for racing; she was conceived as a cruising boat. Heavily built of 2-inch teak planking above the waterline and copper-clad 2 ⅛-inch Oregon and pitch pine below on 4 ¼ x 4-inch oak frames, *Kentra* was designed to cross oceans. She was commissioned by Scottish industrialist Kenneth MacKenzie Clark in 1922 and completed in just six months. Clark's great-grandfather had invented the cotton spinning spool, and his brother sold the family thread manufacturing business in 1896 for £2.5 million, leaving young Kenneth a solid financial legacy—Clark had an estate of over 75,000 acres in Scotland—and plenty of time to indulge in yachts. The name *Kentra* derives from a small township near Acharacle and is the anglicized version of Loch Cann Traigh, or White Sands, where the Vikings may have beached their longboats. Clark also had a motor yacht called *Kentra*. The name has lasted for three quarters of a century, but Clark only kept the S/Y *Kentra* for one season. Some speculate that Clark's wife didn't like the boat; others think that perhaps *Kentra* was not fast enough. Whatever the reason, Clark sold her in a year's time.

Charles Livingston, another Scotsman, had been enamored of *Kentra* when she was under construction and contemplated ordering her sister ship. When he discovered that she was for sale, he purchased

her immediately and sailed her to the Menai Strait, where he kept her from 1924–1936. Livingston, whose family founded the Cunard shipping line, was an inveterate yachtsman, and he used *Kentra* as a base while he raced his one-raters at regattas. Livingston sold *Kentra* a year before he died in 1936 to Barclay Hogarth of the ship owners H. Hogarth & Company for a reputed £3,500. She returned to the Clyde and remained there during the war. During Hogarth's ownership her

The navigation station in the deck saloon, has a fold-down chart table that hides the modern electronic equipment.

The aft cabin has a built-in writing desk flanked by twin berths with matching settes.

petrol/paraffin engine was replaced by diesel. After Hogarth's death, *Kentra* belonged briefly to a Dutchman before being purchased by Major Charles Brassey Thorne, yet another Fife enthusiast. Thorne converted her from a gaff-rigged ketch to a stemhead Bermudian ketch with her bowsprit removed. *Kentra* spent time during these years in Palma and Cannes as a charter boat. Some of her more illustrious guests included Errol Flynn, Brigitte Bardot, and the infanta Cristina of Spain (King Alphonso's daughter). The Thornes gave up the charter business in 1958, and *Kentra* changed hands several times, ending up in the Caribbean. Mr. and Mrs. Cowpland, former owners of *Belle Aventure*, saved her from neglect following a hurricane and did a major refit on her in Antigua. She returned to England in 1983, where she languished for seven years, deteriorating due to lack of funds, until American Vince di Domenica (former owner of *Mariella*) rescued her and brought her to McGruer & Company at Rosneath. Some initial work was done on her hull and a little on her interior. Once again, lack of funds put the project on hold in 1992. *Kentra* was going to go up for auction when a Swiss businessman stepped in to purchase her.

Fairlie Restorations began work on her in October

1993. According to Duncan Walker, *Kentra*'s rebuild was very different from that of *Altair*. Whereas *Altair* had many usable original fittings, *Kentra* needed virtually everything made from scratch. *Kentra* was not originally built to last sixty years. McGruer's had already cast new bronze floors to replace the steel originals. Fairlie renewed 90 percent of the frames below the waterline and 60 percent of those above. The decks were replaced, and new spars and rigging were created. The original skylights and sliding hatch were refitted, and the doghouse was refurbished. The interior layout is the same as it was in 1923; however, there is new mahogany paneling reproduced to look like the old. By all accounts, her original interior was not to the very highest standard. Yet now she is simply elegant. She is, above all, a solid boat, with a wonderfully steady motion. The Swiss couple who own her take pride in sailing *Kentra* to many of the classic yacht events around the Mediterranean and the Caribbean. In addition to *Kentra*, they also own the beautifully restored 8-Meter *Fulmar*. Boats like *Kentra* and *Fulmar* require owners who are passionate about sailing and keen on preserving the past.

The interior, which has been reproduced in the same style, retains the original 1922 layout with only a few minor changes. The main saloon is simple and elegant—the overhead is cream-colored and the paneling is a rich polished red mahogany.

Type: Ketch
LOA: 52' 6" (16 m)
LOD: 43' 4" (13.2 m)
LWL: 35' 5" (10.8 m)
Beam: 14' 6"(4.03 m)
Draft: 5' 5" (1.65 m)
Displacement: 15 tons
Designer: Maurice Amiet
Builder: Jean Boudignon; Arles, France
Year built: 1953
Engine: Diesel 75 cv

LA CLÉ DE SOL

a Clé de Sol was built in 1953 at the Jean Boudignon yard on the Rhone River in Arles, in the south of France. She was designed by Maurice Amiet for Baron Jean de L'Espée. The naval architect of *La Clé* described Jean de L'Espée as an artist, a sympathetic man, extremely sporty, and full of humor. The unique brief for the layout was that it had to accommodate a Steinway baby grand piano. The size of the piano was a major factor in deciding the height and beam of the boat. The baron says: "It is obvious that if I had been 1.70 meters tall and played the flute, the dimensions of the interior space would have been quite different." The yard had never built such a boat before.

The name *La Clé de Sol* (the G Clef) is derived from the baron's love of music. At the age of sixty, the Baron undertook to sail her around the world, fulfilling a life-long ambition. Following her launching, *La Clé* departed from Villefranche in 1954 and made her first transatlantic crossing to Martinique.

After that first crossing, she returned to France on a cargo ship. The second Atlantic crossing was in 1957, which led to a Pacific crossing in 1958 to Tahiti. From 1959 to 1963, she traveled to Hawaii, Japan, Hong Kong, and back to the Mediterranean. On her return to St. Tropez, she had a fantastic

greeting from the Yacht Club of France and French television. In 1964 Jean de L'Espée's ship's log was published under the title *Le Periple de La Clé de Sol*, meaning "the long journey." In addition to his own book, L'Espée wrote about his experience aboard *La Clé de Sol* in *Larousse Nautical Encyclopedia*—a chapter on deep sea cruising in 1965. L'Espée capitalized on his journey through an advertisement in *Bateau* magazine in 1965. In an ad for General Motors, the copy read, "In order to succeed in your world tour as well as Jean de l'Espée, you need a piano, a sailing boat, and a GM Diesel."

*This boat, which was conceived to accommodate a baby grand
piano in the main saloon, is now a liveaboard charter boat.*

The interior layout of La Clé is unique—from the main saloon you can see through to the bow of the boat. The ambience below is one of coziness, comfort, and charm.

Both the galley and the navigation station are compact and functional.

La Clé de Sol is currently owned by an enthusiastic and friendly young French couple, Alain Himgi and Corinne Gantéral, who live aboard and charter the boat in the summers in the Mediterranean. They enjoy following the classic fleet from regatta to regatta, usually hoping to pick up charters. *La Clé* is not as elegant as some, but she has character and spirit!

Type: Motor Yacht
LOA: 159' (48.46 m)
Beam: 28' 9" (8.76 m)
Draft: 10' 5" (3.3 m)
Hull: Steel
Builder/Designer: Botje Ensing & Co.; Holland
Year built: 1965; refitted 1995
Engine: Twin 1020 hp MAN diesel

LAND'S END

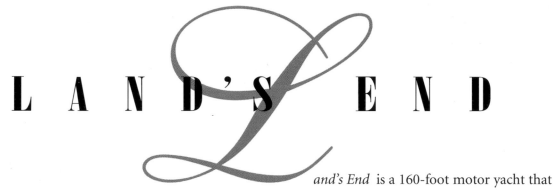

and's End is a 160-foot motor yacht that was built in Holland in 1965 to the specifications of an ocean-going whaler. Her Greek owners used her extensively under the name *Anemos* until they sold her in the early 1970s to Prince Leo of Lignac, who kept her in addition to his 166-foot yacht *Blue Shadow*. Lignac sold both yachts when he took delivery of his 197-foot *New Horizon L*. Her next owner was an American, Bill Bryant, who renamed her *Fantasia* and kept her until 1985, when the Cousteau foundation took over and used her in the Caribbean.

In 1986 she traveled back to Palma, Mallorca and was put on the market. Well-known British yachtsman Peter de Savary bought her and ordered a major refit under the direction of his wife and Jon Bannenberg. He renamed her *Land's End* after the southwest tip of England that he had just acquired to redevelop. De Savary used her in the U.K. and in the Mediterranean until he sold her in 1990. She has since had two French owners who maintained her in top condition as a luxury charter yacht. The

first of these French owners was Oliver Dewavrin, who based her in San Remo. His new captain hired a crew of seven from the Philippines, most of whom are still onboard today. In 1991 *Land's End* went to the Amazon River after a season in the Caribbean. In the spring of 1992 she journeyed back across the Atlantic to Southampton for a refit. Danish Captain Peter Traun took over the boat and did a full summer of chartering in the Mediterranean, including a charter with the Getty family for the Olympics in Spain. In 1993, *Land's End* changed hands again. The latest owner used the boat most of the time himself, with only one outside charter in North Africa, and in 1994 he and his guests did a cruise through Scandinavia. Besides poking in and out of remote harbors, a record number of fish were caught on this trip—the captain

claims one thousand—all of which were eaten! Another highlight of this period was the installation of the Benthos minirover, an underwater remote-control camera (the kind used by Bob Ballard, of Wood's Hole Oceanographic Institute) allowing the guests onboard to enjoy views of the underwater wrecks and fish life at one hundred to two hundred feet. The camera connects to a big TV in the saloon, where people who cannot dive still get a chance to enjoy the underwater world projected on the screen.

Land's End had two refits in 1995, one in Villefranche, and a more extensive one in Marseilles. While *Land's End* is only thirty years old, she maintains a gracious Old-World atmosphere. Her deck area is expansive and comfortable, and her main saloon is open and airy. Forward of the main saloon, the formal dining area is separated by a large etched-glass divider. The cabins are all commodious with en suite bathrooms. There is a definite difference between *Land's End* and modern-day glitzy motor yachts—an air of peace and serenity prevails, and while you never lack for modern conveniences, you still have the impression of Old-World charm.

Type: Schooner
LOA: 83' 10" (25.56 m)
LOD: 74' 10" (22.56 m)
Beam: 16' 8" (5.54 m)
Draft: 9' 6" (3.24 m)
Displacement: 65 tons, approx.
Hull: Iron and steel
Designer: John G. Alden
Builder: Abeking & Rasmussen;
  Lemwerder, Germany
Year built: 1938, Rrefitted 1983, 1995
Engine: GM 179 hp diesel

LELANTINA

Lelantina was awarded the trophy for "the most photogenic yacht" at the 1995 Antigua Classic Yacht Regatta. And there is no doubt that this 85-foot gaff-rigged vessel is about as beautiful a schooner as exists in the world.

The smooth finish on her hull is as impeccable today as it was when she was built, and she still has her original spruce masts. Under her acres of Egyptian-cotton-colored sail (6,600 square feet), she defines grace and balance. John Alden was asked by his client Ralph Peverly—an American living on the Mersey River in Liverpool—to design *Lelanta II* along the same proportions as his 65-foot 1929 *Lelanta*. Like her predecessor, *Lelanta II* was built of steel. Abeking & Rasmussen in Germany were considered the masters of steel construction. *Lelanta II* was launched in 1937.

In the 1950s she was bought by Prince Bihra of Siam, a well-known racing driver. It was he who changed the name from *Lelanta II* to *Lelantina*, a combination of the first names of his three daughters. He sold the boat to an Italian friend, who renovated the interior accommodations. This gentleman only

kept her a short time, quickly turning over the boat to *his* friend Edward Arevian. With Cannes as his home port, Arevian kept her for twenty-two years, taking regular day trips under sail only. Despite his passion for using his boat without an engine; he did install a new GM Diesel.

In 1974 *Lelantina* was bought by a Marseilles shipyard owner, M. Fournier, who, despite a general lack of attention, installed high-quality stainless-steel hardware. Her next owner was M. J. L. Flageul, a French businessman. He sand blasted the hull, did some replating, installed double plates on the bottom, epoxy coated the entire hull, faired the top-sides, and bought new sails, then made a transatlantic voyage. In 1983 she was purchased by Ultramarine and sailed to Denmark, where she

Lelantina's large aft galley has been recently renovated with new cupboards, and a "pass-through" to the dining area.

Once the dishes are washed, they are placed in a cupboard above that drains directly into the sink.

underwent an extensive refit including a new solid teak deck and new accommodation plan. In early 1985 she reappeared in the Mediterranean. In 1989 a syndicate composed of two Parisian parties, Yachting and Communication International, and Philippe LeChevalier, an avid classic yachtsman, bought her and engaged her in the charter trade for five years.

In 1994 she was bought by Monopoly, and a lot of love and care has gone into her, most recently a newly renovated galley. *Lelantina* has joined the fleet of classic yachts that meet periodically at the international classic regattas and events. At the Cannes Régates Royales in 1996, she was stern to the dock alongside a cast of notables. One evening the schooner *Mariette* was hosting a large party at the dock. Two men wandered from the throngs of merrymakers and positioned themselves prostrate on their backs on the

quay abaft of *Lelantina*'s transom, staring out at her. The two men were Peter Woods and Philippe LeChevalier, both of them former owners of *Lelantina*. They were gazing at one of the loves of their lives and reminiscing. Classic yachts do transcend their owners.

Lelantina's *traditional rig belies her almost contemporary interior. From the pilothouse, you can see below to the galley and main saloon.*

The main saloon has an entertainment center and two built-in club chairs to port. An L-shaped leather-upholstered banquette and dining table are to starboard. The table has been nostalgically topped with teak salvaged from Lelantina's original deck.

Type: Marconi Cutter
LOA: 48' (14.63 m)
Beam: 11" (3.35 m)
Draft: 8' (2.44 m)
Displacement: 19 tons
Hull: Teak
Builder: Berthon Boat Works;
   Lymington, England
Year built: 1935, restored 1991

MACNAB

Macnab was designed by Rodney Paul and built in 1935 at Berthon Boat Works in Lymington, England. At the time of her launching she was considered big at 48 feet; she has an 11-foot beam, 8-foot draft, and displaces 19 tons. A Marconi cutter built as a heavy ocean cruiser/racer, she did very well in the Fastnet Race. *Macnab* caught the attention of Charlene Douglas, wife of Bob Douglas, owner/skipper of the Martha's Vineyard icon, the famed yacht *Shenandoah*. The Douglases decided to buy her in 1979 and restore her for use as their personal yacht. She underwent a major rebuild in 1991, which took three years. Her hull is teak, she is copper riveted, and she has new cast bronze floors, frame heels, deck beams, houses, cockpit, and interior. Her unvarnished teak cabin sole was salvaged off a three-master called *Quest. Macnab* was renovated largely by Gary Maynard (owner of *Violet*) at his own yard. Maynard says every aspect of *Macnab* is practical; she is painted one color to the rail caps, and down below she is all varnish (which lasts a long time

below in a cool climate). The mast is aluminum, and the boat can be easily handled by two people.

Below, you can look through from the aft cabin forward. There is a sweet little wood stove, built-in cabinetry, and a place for everything, even wood storage. The odd-shaped doghouse was removed, and a deckhouse over the galley was added to let light into what used to resemble a dark cave. The cockpit was reconfigured, with the wheel replaced by an old-fashioned tiller. Now when the tiller is not in use, it can be tied out of the way, and the cockpit is much roomier. The issue of tiller versus wheel became a marital battle, with Bob favoring the tiller and Charlene wanting to maintain the original wheel. Bob won. The decks are incredibly clean, and the

absence of lifelines makes her sleek and sexy, indeed.

Macnab had been the original name, but when the Douglases bought her she was called *Shoban.* When the King of Greece owned her, she was called *Toxotis III. Macnab* stands out as a pearl among classic yachts. She is just perfect through and through. Bob Douglas is a legend in New England for keeping tradition alive with his schooner, *Shenandoah.* Having a few thoughts about classics, he says, "A classic yacht is obviously a good wooden boat, and the reality is that most were built between the two world wars. Usually only the best materials were used—because as we all know, the best is none too good. White oak and elm frames, double sawn or steam bent, white oak stem and stern posts and keel, yellow pine deck beams, teak planking and decking, planks fastened with copper rivets, deck planking with bronze screws—a boat built this way is good for fifty years. But to maintain her detail and elegance, an owner must rebuild a boat when the time comes. *Macnab* doesn't care whether her owners are British, Portuguese, Greek, German, or American. Even her cruising grounds don't matter; she will survive if she is taken care of. The Vineyard Haven wooden boat fleet is growing—over thirty-five wooden boats call Vineyard Haven home. So wooden boats are not a thing of the past—their numbers are growing, and anyone knows that a good wooden boat can last forever."

On deck, Macnab *is spartan with clean flush decks. Without the obstruction of lifelines and stanchions, she presents a dramatic profile. Having a tiller rather than a wheel allows for more space in the cockpit.*

The galley is small but efficient and bright with overhead hatch, open storage, and stainless steel fixtures.

Below, in contrast to the spare deck, Macnab's *main saloon is rich and sumptuous with burgundy velvet settees, gleaming mahogany paneling, and a cozy fireplace.*

The owner's cabin is quite comfortable and commodious for an aft cockpit boat.

Type: Yawl
LOA: 55' 11" (17.04 m)
LWL: 38' 4" (11.7 m)
Beam: 13' 6" (4.11 m)
Draft: 5' 3" (1.6 m)
Displacement: 45,312 lbs. (20, 596 kg)
Hull: Mahogany on oak
Designer: Sparkman & Stephens
Builder: Mattiessen & Paulsen; Germany
Year built: 1959

MAGIC CARPET

Magic Carpet was commissioned by a Peter Richmond from Connecticut in 1959. She was designed by Sparkman & Stephens and built by Mattiessen & Paulson in Germany (a small yard, the caliber of Abeking & Rasmussen). In her inaugural year she won the Marblehead–to–Halifax race. Much as he loved her, Richmond only owned *Magic Carpet* for a year, before losing her in a divorce settlement.

The two subsequent owners were from New England, as well. Charles Robe from Connecticut used her as a family cruising boat, then sold her to Bruce Steer from Harwichport, Massachusetts. Steer owned her for seventeen years—cruising New England in the summers and using her out of Palm Beach in the winters. Steer, now in his 80s, has fond memories of his boat. She went to the Caribbean once but was mostly used as a coastal day sailor.

Lee Taylor and Tod Bassett of Martha's Vineyard, Massachusetts, are the sixth owners of *Magic Carpet*. They both grew up around boats and sailing and had a firm vision of their ideal boat. They purchased her in 1995 to live aboard and run day charters out of Edgartown in the summers. They find that in sailing around *Magic Carpet*'s old haunts, a lot of people who are familiar with her stop by to fill them in on episodes in her life.

She is sturdily built—diagonally bronze strapped with Monel floors. The spars and decks are original, but the cabin top was fiberglassed over in the '80s. In 1989 the hull, which is double-planked mahogany, was 80 percent replaced at Billings Yard in Deer Isle, Maine.

Lee and Tod feel she is perfect for charter. All the sheets are fed aft, and the large, comfortable cockpit is uncluttered. An ample cockpit locker enables them to keep all the sails out of the fore-

Magic Carpet *charters out of Martha's Vineyard in the summer, and is always popular as a competitor in the Opera House Cup Race in Nantucket.*

peak and separate engine room. With her centerboard, *Magic Carpet* only draws 5½ feet.

The interior is roomy, light and well ventilated—a Sparkman & Stephens trademark. With bronze hardware, the boat has the look and the feel of a classic. Lee Taylor has a predilection for the 1940s style so that while there is a yachty, nautical feel below, the interior is distinctively different because of her wildly floral print fabrics and curtains. Adding to the charm are the funky lampshades, the homey galley, and the birdcage in the main saloon. Gus, a friendly cockatiel, is a full-fledged member of the crew and adds life, color and melody to this liveaboard boat.

Finally, *Magic Carpet* is aptly named, as she sails well. She is a great reacher, moving effortlessly at 10 knots, and a forestay can be rigged handily if they want more sail opportunities. Lee and Tod are *real* sailors and it appears as if they have a *real* sailing boat!

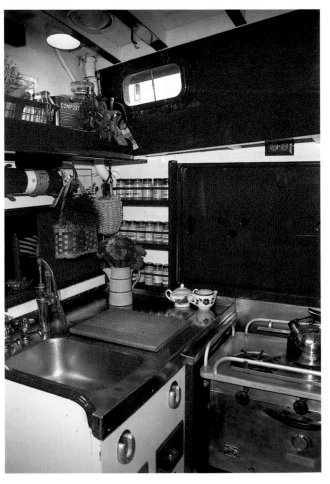

Belowdecks, Magic Carpet *shows the care and style of liveaboard owners. The interior is distinctively different. The mix of navy blue setees and '40s floral print fabric is creative and fun while still maintaing a nautical feel.*

The galley is small, but cheerful and efficient with sink and stove to port and refrigerator to starboard. Everything is in reach with a lot of open storage space.

The aft cabin has two large single bunks divided by a settee and dresser.

Gus, a friendly cockatiel, is a full-fledged member of the crew.

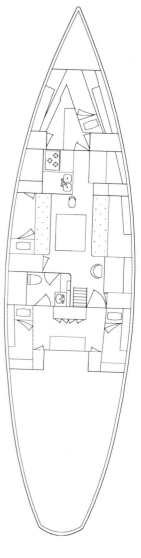

Type: Schooner
LOA: 138' (42.06 m)
LOD: 108' 2" (33 m)
LWL: 80' (24.38 m)
Beam: 23' 7" (7.19 m)
Draft: 14' 6" (4.42 m)
Displacement: 165 tons
Hull: Steel
Designer/Builder: Nathaniel Herreshoff;
  Maine, U.S.A
Year built: 1915; restoration; 1995
Engine: Twin GM 6-71, 6-cyl. 185 hp diesels

MARIETTE

ariette is without a doubt one of the finest schooners that Nathaniel Herreshoff ever built. Commissioned by Bostonian Frederick Brown, she was launched in 1915 with much fanfare. She was prominent in the yachting news because she was a close sister to Harold Vanderbilt's famous yacht (his second) *Vagrant*. Her actual sister ship was *Ohonkara*, owned by Karl L. Tucker (this schooner, later named *Ramona*, had a tragic demise in the waters off Bermuda). Brown kept *Mariette* for over ten years; when he was ready to sell, an eager buyer was in the wings. Francis "Keno" Crowninshield had long been an admirer of *Mariette* and was able to purchase her in 1927. He chose to rename her *Cleopatra's Barge II*, in honor of one of the first yachts built in America in 1816 by his ancestor. Legend has it that the first *Cleopatra's Barge* sailed across the Atlantic to help Napoleon depose the pope. Crowninshield kept his beloved yacht until 1941, at which time she was requisitioned by the U.S. Coast Guard and used as a patrol boat for the duration of World War II.

After the war, with her condition much deteriorated, Crowninshield reluctantly sold her.

Her third owner called her *Gee Gee IV*. The '50s and '60s were not an auspicious time for this grand yacht, for she went through a succession of owners who did not seem to cherish and take care of her. In the '70s, she was purchased by a Canadian, Walter Boudreau, and brought to the Caribbean. He renamed her *Janeen*, after his oldest daughter, and operated her as a charter boat out of his hotel in Marigot, St. Lucia. In 1975 Boudreau sold her to a group of Italian and Swiss bankers.

In 1979 Italian publisher Alberto Rizzoli bought her and hired Eric Pascoli to help rebuild her under the guidance of Ugo Faggioni at

Mariette's rig, deck configuration, and fittings were largely transformed in 1995. A steering cockpit which was not part of the original design was added, and fittings were cast in nickel aluminum bronze to replace the ill-matched stainless-steel ones.

Cantieri Beconcini in La Spezia. Her original interior was significantly restored at this time, and she was given her original name back. Nonetheless, she was transformed with an updated staysail rig and a new deck configuration. The Rizzolis kept her quite a few years, sailing her around their favorite anchorages in the Mediterranean, until they finally sold her. *Mariette* was in need of a new patron, and as fate would have it, Tom Perkins, a California inventor and businessman, was searching for a unique classic yacht. Initially he was captivated by the Alden schooner *Puritan*, but ultimately he was unable to buy her. At the 1994 Nioulargue Race, he observed *Mariette*'s sailing ability and was intrigued. Having been involved with sailing all his life (he owns a 154-foot Perini Navi ketch *Andromeda la Dea*), he wanted a classic he could race. An inveterate yachtsman, he has raced a variety of yachts and was keen on being a hands-on owner; *Mariette* had found an owner dedicated to her restoration. Tom Eaton (who had been *Puritan*'s skipper for years as well as supervisor of her restoration) was hired to be the skipper and project manager of *Mariette*'s rebuild.

The rebuild of *Mariette* went much the same way as that of *Altair*. Massive research was undertaken; over 150 drawings depicting rig and deck plans were obtained from the Hart Collection at M.I.T. in Massachussetts, where Herreshoff had studied. A major restructuring of her rig to the original configuration was completed by Harry Spencer. He shipped new spars to the Beconcini yard in Italy. Ratsey made the special cream-colored sails for the new rig. All fittings were cast in nickel aluminum bronze by Wessex Castings. Along with an entirely new rig, she underwent a completely renovated deck plan. Old stainless-steel fittings were replaced with new lustrous ones designed by Tom Eaton and cast by Oscar Genesi. A steering cockpit aft was a new addition; because the

The master stateroom includes a private study, furnished with a red leather settee.

The bathroom with a wood-trimmed bathtub must have been quite a luxury when Mariette was built.

The tiled fireplace was custom-designed for Mariette *in Ireland.*

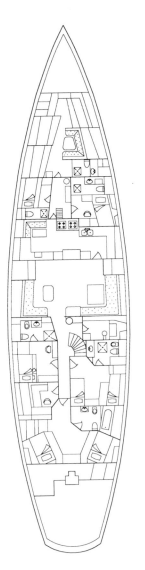

owner is normally at the helm, his guests can sit in comfort and safety nearby. The other cockpit forward of the helm is an old modification of the original. *Mariette*'s deck gleams with tradition and reflects love and care.

Belowdecks is extraordinary. The main saloon spans the entire beam of the boat. Her lustrous paneling is the original Russian walnut. To port is an L-shaped lounge area with settees and armchairs upholstered in a rich red leather. Closed-cupboard bookshelves and exquisite built-in cabinets showcase rare books, china, and various trophies. The tiled fireplace, created for *Mariette* in the summer of 1996 in Ireland, is both beautiful and incredibly efficient. A writing desk is on the aft starboard bulkhead and the commodious dining area is all the way to starboard. Beautiful seventeenth-and eighteenth-century oil

paintings, for the most part nautical subjects, adorn the bulkheads. A fifteenth-century ceramic plate called the Armatore is one of Perkins's favorite pieces. In a cupboard is an old yacht trophy from 1848—the first trophy of the America's Cup dates from 1851. An ornate silver tureen sitting atop a breakfront has a story. When Perkins bought *Mariette*, he asked to purchase the tureen. Wolf Chitis, *Mariette*'s former owner, told him it was a priceless family heirloom; he couldn't sell it, but he would be happy to make a gift of it to the yacht.

Beauty surrounds *Mariette*—below, on deck, and under sail. Seen from the dock in Monte Carlo, Cannes, or St. Tropez, this noble schooner makes a stunning impression. Her deck and interior are without equal—and to sail this incredible schooner is an unforgettable experience.

The main saloon with its original lustrous walnut paneling and cabinetry has been thoroughly refurbished. It spans the entire beam of the boat; to port is an L-shaped lounge area with settees and armchairs, and to starboard is the dining area. Red leather settees, antique silver and eighteenth-century oil paintings add to the richness of the room.

Type: Motor Yacht, Commuter
LOA: 62' (18.9 m)
Beam: 11' 5" (3.5 m)
Draft: 3' 6" (1.1 m)
Hull: Mahogany on oak
Builder: Consolidated Ship Building;
 Morris Heights, N.Y.
Year built: 1923, Rebuilt 1988–1990
Engine: Twin Palmer Gas Engines

MISS ASIA

iss Asia, under the original name *Margaret F*, was built in 1923 by the Consolidated Ship Building Corporation of Morris Heights, New York, for Lawrence P. Fisher of Fisher Auto Body Works in Detroit. Fisher used his yacht as a means of commuting to work on the Detroit River. She is the earliest example of the Speedway series of commuter yachts. Two years after she was launched, Fisher went on to build another yacht and sold her. In succession her name changed to *Lura M. II*, then to *Alalba*, and in 1927 she was bought by J. Frederick Byers and renamed *Bing*. Byers used her mainly out of Watch Hill, Rhode Island, until he sold her in the mid 1930s. Some early Rosenfeld photographs were taken at the Yale/Harvard Crewing events under Byers's ownership.

Bing changed hands several times and was based in New York, Boston, Key West, and Miami. In 1960 John Astor bought her in Miami and renamed her *Miss Asia*. In 1962 her official home port was

New York, but she continued to move up and down the East Coast. In 1973 Astor's daughter Jacqueline took over the boat and actually lived on her for a couple of years in Palm Beach and Ft. Lauderdale. Her next owner was W. Haden Judsen Jr. from Philadelphia, who kept her until 1987. She is now owned by Gary Conover, who found her in Essex, Connecticut. He had her rebuilt extensively at Essex Boat Works over a period of years. Conover also owns the lovely Charlotte Inn in Edgartown on Martha's Vineyard. His yacht mirrors his inn in terms of exquisite taste and uncanny attention to detail. The hull is mahogany on oak frames but has been fiberglassed. She used to be black but is now painted white. Renovations have been ongoing. Original engines were Speedways, now she has twin Palmer gas engines.

Miss Asia *has the distinct lines of a 1920s commuter.*
She has been exquisitely renovated and is maintained
in Bristol condition by her owner, Martha's Vineyard
hotelier, Gary Conover.

Her interior wood paneling is original. The decks have been replaced, and her galley has been renovated. The microwave has been thrown out and a period copper-lined icebox was installed. The flooring in the head and galley were a poor imitation parquet, and the tile was an offensive powder blue. Conover tracked down a source for 1920s linoleum to revamp the head and the galley, replacing the tile. All the fixtures, upholstery, and appointments are totally in keeping with her original style and era.

Miss Asia was used as a VIP boat for the 1989 J Class Race between *Shamrock* and *Endeavour*. She was also hostess to Princess Di during her stay on Martha's Vineyard. *Miss Asia* simply gleams with well-maintained brightwork, as well as obvious devotion and love. Gary Conover is the perfect caretaker of a classic yacht.

Whatever was not original down below, was researched and recreated in the style and period of the 1920s. The result is a beautifully appointed interior that mirrors the attention to detail so evident on deck.

Type: Cutter
LOA: 59' (17.9 m)
LOD: 53' 5" (16.28 m)
LWL: 40' (12.19 m)
Beam: 10' 6" (10.80 m)
Draft: 7' 8" (2.33 m)
Displacement: 41,000 lbs.
Hull: Original yellow pine on red oak
  (rebuilt mahogany on white oak)
Designer: Nathaniel G. Herreshoff
Builder: Bristol, Rhode Island
Year built: 1907;
  Restored: 1980-82, 1983-85, 1993
Engine: 1993 Yanmar 50 hp

NEITH

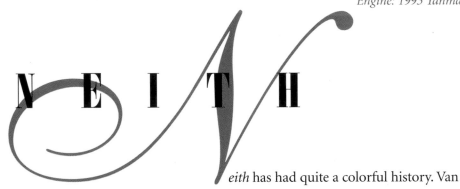

*N*eith has had quite a colorful history. Van Brown, the son of the current owner, tells the wonderful tale of *Neith's* ninety years: A gaff cutter, she was built in 1907 as a weekender for Nathaniel Herreshoff's personal physician, Dr. Ed Dunham. In those days, a Herreshoff sailboat—61 feet overall, 53 feet on deck, with a narrow 10½-foot beam—cost $9,000. *Neith* was built like most Herreshoffs of the day with double-planked topsides, fir over cypress, yellow pine bottom planking, white pine or fir decks, and spruce spars. The standard choices for the interior were butternut or cypress, varnished or painted white, trimmed out with mahogany. Upholstery was covered with red or green velvet or leather.

Sold to her third owner in 1919, *Neith* became famous in 1920–21 for sailing across the Atlantic. On

her first attempt in 1920, she was driven back by storms. She spent the winter in Halifax. In 1921, after "chopping her rig off" and making her into a stubby gaff yawl, *Neith* set off again. This time she made it to England. *Yachting* magazine did a four-part story on the adventure. Five men sailing across the Atlantic in a "small" boat like *Neith* was exciting news in the 1920s. There were even entertaining hand-cranked films of *Neith* arriving in England; Mortimer Gordon, the boat's cook, is featured, pretending to ladle out stew onto the deck.

Neith spent most of her life in Scotland and England. With her shortened yawl rig, she was slow in anything but a gale. Stories about the boat have Charles Nicholson, the famous yacht designer, convincing the owner in 1926 to try the new Marconi-style rig. Nicholson's distinctive rig was very successful and stands in *Neith* today. Nicholson later may have regretted that he made *Neith* so fast. In his

Neith is fast, sleek and quite competitive in her class. In her early years she went from a tall gaff cutter to a "stubby" gaff yawl. In 1926, Charles Nicholson designed a new Marconi style rig which stands in her today.

autobiography, he wrote that during one of the Fastnet races, he saw a storm coming and shortened his sails. The rest of the fleet was slow to react and was blown away. When the storm cleared, he said, "Once again, there was that damned *Neith*, close on my quarter."

Neith has always attracted colorful owners. Although a South African owner continued to keep her in Scotland, he would often sail her back to South Africa with an all-girl crew. Today *Neith's* professional crew is again all female.

Maybe *Neith* is more comfortable with women. After all, Neith is the Egyptian Goddess of the Hunt. At one time a Scots owner kept a small ancient bronze of the goddess. At the beginning of every season, a raucous party took the statue from the hearth in his house, and—with bagpipes skirling—Neith was installed on the boat. At the end of season, with much fanfare, the process was reversed.

A great part of *Neith's* story has been about sur-

vival. Over the span of her life, her bowsprit has become shorter and shorter until finally, in the 1950s, she became a stemhead rig. Sixty years of hard sailing in some of the roughest waters of the world, numerous transatlantics, and trips to South Africa finally took their toll. *Neith* was laid up to die.

Then in the late '60s, a progressive and experimental program at Michigan State University let four college boys receive eighteen hours of credit for bumming around—"studying"—the culture of the ports and harbors of Europe. Looking for cheap transportation and lodging, they came across a tired-looking black hulk rotting in Scotland—*Neith*. She was in sad shape, with her rig moss covered and lying in a distant field. Fortunately, the boys from Michigan were completely naive about boats. They bought her for £2,750.

Truly not knowing a thing about sailing, the foursome got a sixteen-year-old boy who supposedly "knew how to sail" to teach them how. They assembled the scattered bits and pieces of this old boat and got her ready to go to sea once again. Neither the callow owners nor their tutor knew much about boats, and when the mast was stepped, they thought that it had either shrunk or that it had worn and enlarged the "hole" in the deck. None of them realized that mast wedges were needed to hold the mast in place. Thus rigged, it was time to go to sea.

Off went these innocents into the teeth of an English Channel gale—without lights, engine, pumps, charts, compass, or knowledge. The current carried them to and fro, and miraculously landed them at their intended destination in France. "Hey, this sailing stuff is easy!" they decided. Around they turned, and the tides carried them to and fro, and once again a miracle happened. The five boys were back in their home port, where they were promptly arrested by the Coast Watch of England for going to sea in an unsafe craft.

Equipped with the barest minimum of lights, prewar charts, and relying on a Sea Scout manual to teach them about boats, the boys, now just three, set out to explore Europe. Confident that eventually they would figure out navigation, they sailed to France, across the treacherous Bay of Biscay to Portugal, and on to Spain. "If there's land on the left side, we must still be going South," they reasoned.

One time, tired and hungry, after the out-of-date charts and their weak dead reckoning failed them, they decided that they had to make a port call. A harbor entrance beckoned. In Neith roared at ten knots, only to discover too late that there was no room to turn around in the tiny harbor. Neith thudded into the mud. Down went the hook. Safe. Now where were they? Ever resourceful, one of the boys hailed another boat. He told the fellow cruisers that he was making the log entry, and "what was the correct spelling of this port?"

The port name meant nothing to the intrepid crew, but the lights of town called to them. When ashore, they were presented with a chain-link fence, crowds, and lots of noise. A party! No gate was offered so they climbed the fence, dropped into the street, and found themselves in the middle of a running of the bulls!

Eventually Neith made it to Mallorca for a refit. The boys were ready to sail her back to the United States. An old sea captain, about to depart on a freighter, would not have been able to live with his conscience if he had not helped them get home safely. To help them on their way, and perhaps be able to sleep at night, he gave them his own sextant. What a luxury to know exactly where they were!

In 1971 Neith made a slow crossing to Antigua in the West Indies. The boys left her in Antigua until the next year, when they sailed her back to her birthplace in New England. That summer they cruised her to Marblehead Harbor. There they were able to get past the formidable presence of Mrs. Brown, L. Francis Herreshoff's housekeeper, and met L. Francis, the son of Nathaniel Herreshoff, himself. He told the boys that he had watched them sail into Marblehead and immediately recognized the boat as Neith. He said that Neith was the very first boat that his father had ever let him work on. A year after this meeting, L. Francis died.

It was time for the boys to get on with their lives. Neith was again in rough shape, and she was sold and moved to Old Saybrook, Connecticut. Her new owner

Jack Brown at the helm of Neith *in the 1996 Opera House cup in Nantucket, Massachusetts.*

Her deck is clean and unobstructed. During her restoration, new bronze fittings were machined, special bronze winches were ordered and new blocks were made from lignum vitae.

was involved with a project in Central America but had left money and instructions with a yard to care for *Neith*. However, a clerical error made the yard think that she was unpaid for. She was tied to a floating dock with only tires for fenders and left to languish.

The sight of this beautiful yacht slowly being lost moved many people. The individuals who eventually formed the Museum of Yachting did so in large part because of the sad fate of *Neith*. They decided that they would try to find a way so that other great boats would not be lost to neglect.

Neith began to die at her dock. The tires would work away from her hull, and the hard concrete dock cut into her side. Without pumps it was only a matter of time until the end came. Finally, a heavy rain filled her through her open hatches until she settled to the holes worn in her hull.

On Christmas Day 1979, *Neith* sank into the Connecticut River.

Others could not stand by and see her lost. One was Elizabeth Hersant. Once again, *Neith* had to be saved. Elizabeth and her husband, Doug, tracked down the owner to Belize and learned that he would be flying back to the United States in two days. When the owner got off the jet in Florida he was met by a very cooperative state trooper—who had him call the Hersants. When he was told about his boat, he agreed to sell her to Elizabeth and Doug, but for a non-negotiable price: one quibble and the deal was off. The Hersants did not quibble. Elizabeth always said that *Neith* was Doug's present.

The Hersants and a group of friends raised *Neith* and nursed her back to Mystic. Once again her charmed life took effect. Two of the best young boat builders in the area began to restore *Neith*. No one had ever started with less. *Neith* was worn, broken, and battered. She got new hull planking and decks, covering boards, toe rail, and king plank. Frames were sistered, and new ceiling planking was installed. New strapping was laid into her hull and decks. Her Herreshoff iron hanging knees were rebuilt. Her stern was rebuilt and strengthened.

Although hollow and engineless, the Hersants took her sailing. They put in an appearance at the Herreshoff Museum's Rendezvous and that summer took home a well deserved Best Restoration Award.

The start is the most important part of a yacht restoration project because once she is saved, others may take up the work to finish her. So it was this time. *Neith's* unique flat, yellow-pine bowsprit was the last gift the Hersants had to give to their friend *Neith*. Once more, she was on the market, and continued to deteriorate.

A local yacht broker, one of the original group that had brought *Neith* to Mystic, set out to save *Neith* once again. He took Van Brown to look at *Neith* again and again, but Brown had a hard time seeing what the appeal of this moldering hulk was. Her hulls were dingy gray from sitting next to a railway bridge. The decks looked like moss or mildew was growing on them. Her decrepit interior held only a hammock, some empty wine bottles, and a porta potty.

Slowly, the training and friendship that had been extended to him by Mystic Seaport Museum and the people of the area won Brown over. If this old hulk (that's how she looked even though almost new) was important to all these people, then it would be important to him.

She could never be his, but his father—Jack Brown, of Midland, Texas—had recently become interested in yachting. However, Jack liked modern, fast, fiberglass boats and had just purchased one the year before. Needless to say, he couldn't understand why his son wanted him to become involved with a boat that needed so much work.

Van kept taking his father to the sad-looking *Neith*. Slowly, she started weaving her old spell. Van kept telling Jack how important *Neith* was. Finally, more in frustration than anything else, Jack asked, "If she's so important, why doesn't somebody else save her?" Van replied, "Maybe they just can't see how it could be done." After a moment's pause, Jack Brown said, "Well, if no one else will do it, maybe we should."

Jack Brown had two objectives. One, that she must be restored as original and to equal or better quality than original, and two, that all the modern conveniences must be in place but unseen. Not easy, perhaps never done before, but it was a deal.

The restoration of *Neith* made the Browns part of a very committed community. Boatyards made places for them. Old photos were found to help them. M.I.T. helped locate all the old Herreshoff drawings.

It's all done now. New frames and floors, new mast step, refastened throughout, new floor-to-frame bolts, new interior, a copper-lined shower worked into some unused space, new electrical, new reefer box, modern electronics hidden in the old liquor cabinet, lost drawings of her original table found and made into a piece of art, custom gimbaled stove, new tanks, engine, pumps, rigging, sails, cushions, mattresses, library carvings redone from one found but shattered piece, new bronze machined fittings, blocks made from lignum vitae and special-order bronze winches—every last piece special because hundreds of people wanted her to have the best. This devotion cannot be asked for; it can only be given.

The interior is painted a typical Herreshoff white and trimmed with varnished mahogany. The settees are upholstered in a moss green tufted-velvet. All modern electronics are hidden in an old liquor cabinet.

Did the Browns always plan to make *Neith* into what she is today? Van thinks that all the people in this area who cared so much about this boat "guided" them. The work that was done on each portion was so exceptional that to put anything less than extraordinary next to it would look out of place.

They were fortunate to draw the very best that the area had to offer. Many put aside careers just to be part of this restoration; one of these was an extremely talented woodworker, a Ph.D. who was teaching philosophy at the state university. Van knew him to be a great talent when working with wood. He bid, along with several others, to do the deck furniture (houses, skylights, and so on). When Van found out that the low bidder did not know how to do dovetails, he awarded the job to the philosopher. He remembers laughing with him about how the low bidder, though not knowing how to do dovetails, had had the brass to bid on the job. The philosopher laughed right along with him. Still chuckling, he went home—and spent all night learning and perfecting dovetail joinery.

Has it been worth it? There is no feeling like sitting at a dock and having an elderly gentleman recognize *Neith* as his favorite boat from 1912. Or have a woman stop to tell about being a young girl and nanny on the yacht when *Neith* first came to the U.S. Or sail across Narragansett Bay and be hailed from afar: "Is that *Neith*? I sailed on her when I was a boy in Scotland." The Browns have even had the children of her old European owners come visit her to see how she is getting on.

Saving and owning a yacht like *Neith* makes the Browns a part of this history. They are, like others who own classic yachts, only the caretakers of these boats. But what a grand thing it is to enjoy them for awhile before passing the torch on to others.

Her interior was carefully rebuilt with extreme attention to detail.
Original drawings helped ensure that the dining table was constructed just right. Even the library carvings were replicated from
one shattered piece that was found.

Type: Motor Yacht
LOA: 83' (25.29 m)
Beam: 18' 1" (5.51 m)
Draft: 8' 6" (2.59 m)
Displacement: 90 tons
Hull: Pine on double-sawn frames
Builder: Newbert & Wallace Yard;
 Thomaston, Maine
Year built: 1948;
 restored 1989 (Rockland, Maine)

PAULINE

auline, now an elegant mahogany-paneled charter boat, belies her salty, humble origins. She was built in 1948 at the Newbert and Wallace Yard in Thomaston, Maine, as a sardine carrier to service the North Lubec Canning Company at its Rockland plant. Designer/builder Roy Wallace built several sardine carriers and draggers between 1947 and 1952. They were constructed with 4-inch double-sawn frames and 2-inch hard-pine planking. They all had three watertight bulkheads, with the engine room in the aft compartment and the living quarters up forward. The two holds amidships carried the fish. Captain Henry Dodge and his mate/cook Carl "Swede" Carlson operated *Pauline* for almost twenty years alongside a purse seiner. When the sun went down, the schooling herring came to the surface and were encircled and trapped by the purse seine before being pumped aboard the *Pauline*. She was always kept like a yacht—very clean and pristine—and was known up and down the coast as "the beautiful *Pauline*." Cook Swede always had a pot of chowder on the stove and a glass of rum for whoever came by.

In 1988–89 Ken and Ellen Barnes (who also own the schooner *Stephen Taber*) bought *Pauline* and designed and enabled the retrofit. They were concerned as to how the fisherman would take to *Pauline* being transformed into a motor yacht, but they are pleased that they have been told that she looks great. The sardine industry is dead, and Maine fishermen know it's tough to make a living on the sea. The builder, Roy Wallace, when he was in his late eighties, saw *Pauline* from the dock, came aboard, and commended the Barneses on a job well done.

The Barneses removed the old pilothouse and took everything down to the deck level, creating a charter boat for twelve guests, with six equal staterooms. In each cabin is a bureau, hanging locker, and a sink. The

Pauline *was operated as a working sardine carrier until she was purchased by Ellen and Ken Barnes and rebuilt as a charter boat in 1988/1989. She remains as solid and as strong as ever, and moves easily through the waters off the coast of Maine.*

The deck saloon, similar to a large English parlor, offers several inviting seating areas. Fabrics for curtains and pillows were purchased from estate sales to create the atmosphere of turn-of-the century elegance.

bathrooms and showers are outside the cabins. The doors on the deck saloon are South American cedar, but the balance of the woodwork is Honduran mahogany. For cold evenings there is a cozy wood-burning fireplace. The rest of the decor is turn of the century—the damask fabric on the couches is Victorian as are the crewel pillows and other appointments such as china and silver that were purchased at estate auctions to create the gracious-ness of the golden age of yachting. In the pilot house, they were able to use the wheel, binnacle, radar, and fish finder from the sardine carrier. Two pieces of art in the main saloon—a framed sardine carton and a shadow box with three cans of sar-dines—are reminders of her roots.

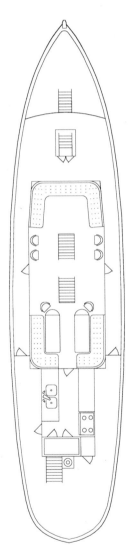

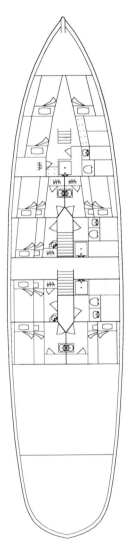

The wheelhouse is simply configured, like that of a tug boat, with ample visibility.

The on-deck galley is utilitarian and efficient for serving gourmet charter meals for twelve guests three times a day—and of course, at tea time.

Type: Diesel Cruiser
LOA: 96' (29.26 m)
Beam: 18' 3" (5.56 m)
Draft: 8' (2.43 m)
Displacement: 135 tons
Hull: Douglas fir
Designer: L. E. "Ted" Geary
Builder: Lake Union Dry Dock
  and Machine Works; Seattle, Wash.
Year built: 1928; restored 1994
Engine: D343 Caterpillar Diesel D-343

PRINCIPIA

rincipia was the heaviest diesel yacht ever built in the Pacific Northwest when she was launched in 1928. Designed by M.I.T.-trained naval architect L. E. "Ted" Geary for Californian L. A. Macomber, she was built at the Lake Union Dry Dock & Machine Works in Seattle, Washington. Macomber was purportedly chairman of the board at Principia College, thus the name. Geary designed three close sister ships, *Blue Peter* being the most famous—she was of the same style but powered with twin 175 hp gasoline engines instead of one 240 hp Atlas Imperial diesel. The other two yachts, *Electra* and *Canim*, twin screw diesel-driven boats, were launched in 1930.

Principia was designed to cruise at 11 knots and carry fuel for a 4,000-mile radius. Macomber cruised her in Alaska in the summer and California and Mexico in the winter. According to an article in *Pacific Motorboat* magazine from April 1928, "Her frames are doubled of four-inch flitch, her planking is of three-inch material, and her scantlings are in proportion. The top timbers of the frames and

bulwarks are of Alaskan cedar to resist dry rot, and in addition the boat has been thoroughly salted."

The year she was launched was the last of an era of boat building, the last time to display new wealth. Black Friday, the fateful day on Wall Street when the stock market crashed in 1929, put a halt to the pleasure craft market for a while. During the succeeding years, streamlining became prevalent in all new construction. *Principia* is a true classic. Built right before the crash, she was constructed of the finest materials and has stately proportions and traditional detailing.

Like so many pleasure craft at the time of World War II, *Principia* was conscripted by the U.S. Coast Guard as fire patrol vessel, CG-914F. In 1946 she was purchased by Karl G. Hurd and based in Tacoma,

Principia *was built in 1928 in the Pacific Northwest as a custom pleasure craft just prior to the Great Depression. After a colorful checkered history, her restoration was completed in 1994 at Billings Diesel and Marine in Stonington, Maine. Her original appearance with her two masts and smokestack was replicated.*

The idea was to repair, upgrade, and restore Principia *to what she was like at her inception, but at the same time bring her up to Coast Guard certification. The wheelhouse maintains the classic feel, but has modern electronic equipment added.*

Washington, for two years. From 1949–1955 she was owned by Alf Mason, who used her to house bear hunters in Alaska. During that time, appropriately enough, her name was changed to *Kodiak Bear*. Between 1956–1961 she returned to Seattle, and her new owners, Mr. and Mrs. Toyah Sager, reinstated her original name. From 1962–1966 *Principia* had a few different owners but remained in the Seattle area. In 1967 John Fenz bought her and home ported her in Sausalito, California. From 1975–1993 the entertainer John Davidson, (*Hollywood Squares*) owned her. He brought her down the California coast to San Diego and eventually took her on a family cruise through the Panama Canal to Ft. Lauderdale. Although Davidson loved and used her often, she fell into disrepair after she was left unattended in Ft. Lauderdale.

The Independence Seaport Museum in Philadelphia had been on the search for a true classic worthy of restoration, and in 1993 their representative made an offer of $112,000—good for three hours. The offer was accepted. Anticipating a major refit, the museum's director organized a plan to restore her at the Billings Diesel and Marine Yard in

Stonington, Maine. With Harlan Billings, owner of the yard, onboard, she made the 1,500 mile trip north at a steady 10 knots without stopping and without damage. The Independence Seaport Museum obtained the original drawings from the Smithsonian Institute and set about doing as much research on *Principia* as possible. The idea was to repair, upgrade, and restore *Principia* to what she was like at her inception, but at the same time bring her up to Coast Guard certification to be able to charter and carry passengers. In deference to the look of the era, John Davidson's foredeck Jacuzzi was summarily removed. The museum wanted to duplicate everything right to scale. The spars are brand new as is the foredeck hatch and the smokestack. Wiring and plumbing are all brand new. The hull is mostly original, but the deck handrails had to be raised to meet Coast Guard standards. For the same reason, the back doors—which are cargo doors mounted on a frame—were added. All of the interior is new; somewhere in her previous history, twin staterooms were converted to make one large master stateroom. The main saloon has been decorated to conform to the era in which she was conceived. The house has been extended over the years but fits gracefully at this juncture. In 1995 Macomber's grandson unexpectedly came to view the boat because his mother had always talked about her and especially about the fireplace. To his dismay, the fireplace had long since been torn out, probably when the military had it. Unfortunately, the captain never got Macomber's address or phone number to ask additional questions.

A large part of what makes yacht restoration so interesting, beyond the layers of varnish and paint, are the stories and people who have passed through the life of a yacht, particularly one that is almost seventy years old. It is to the Independence Seaport Museum's credit that it had the wherewithal to purchase and restore *Principia*.

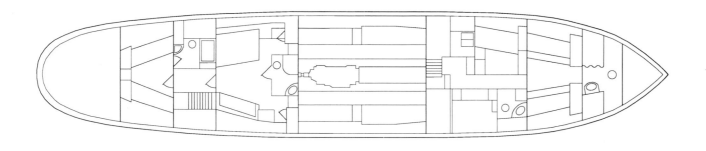

The main saloon depicts the essence of the era of the Golden Age of American yachting. She is replete with varnished woods, brass, bronze, and etched leaded glass.

For a large boat, she only accommodates four guests in two luxurious staterooms. One double has a queen-size berth and the other has twin beds. Both have en suite bathrooms.

Type: Schooner
LOA: 102' 9" (31.32 m)
LWL: 74' 8" (22.77 m)
Beam: 22' 10" (6.7 m)
Draft: centerboard up 9' (2.74 m)
Displacement: 140 tons
Hull: Steel
Designer: John G. Alden
Builder: Electric Boat Company;
 Groton, Connecticut
Year built: 1931; restored 1972; refit 1990

P U R I T A N

Puritan is considered one of the prettiest schooners John Alden ever designed. Alden was commissioned to draw the plans for the boat by H. J. Curtis in 1929. According to the story, he had just finished drawing the plans when the phone rang. Told it was his client, Curtis, Alden assumed that Curtis wanted once again to modify or change some part of the plans. However, the phone call was to inform him that the market had crashed on Wall Street; his client was ruined and would not be able to even consider owning a yacht. Alden only had to worry for a few days about this turn of events because another member of the New York Yacht Club, Edward M. Brown, called him, wanting to assume the plans. But, even before Alden finalized his new modifications, Brown, too, reneged. Due to the Depression, he was no longer in a position to carry on with *Puritan*.

Finally a Californian, Henry J. Bauer, was the one to actually assume delivery of *Puritan* at the Electric Boat Company in New London, Connecticut, in mid-April 1931. *Puritan* sailed from Groton in April 1933. It was an inauspicious time for the American economy: Roosevelt had been inaugurated as president, and on March 6 he closed the nation's banks. Groton and New London were disaster areas. Still, *Puritan* made her trip to California through the Panama Canal. Bauer was fanatical about her

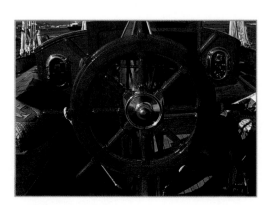

upkeep. All the outside brightwork was always covered by a dust cloth, and he revarnished the boat three times a year!

The accommodation plan for *Puritan* was lavish. The owner's stateroom aft extended the full beam of the boat. The companionway, with its gleaming mahogany handrail, led to a corridor off of which were the guest staterooms port and starboard. Each cabin had a private bathroom with enamel tub and shower, dispensing hot and cold fresh as well as salt water. The main saloon and dining area forward

with some of the work being done at the Lido Shipyard. When she was finished, Bauer took *Puritan* to Baja California, stopping in every harbor of interest, looking for shells, artifacts, marine life, and birds. Bauer, an amateur naturalist, hired a writer to chronicle his findings, and *Puritan* stayed in Mexican waters for two months. She was also used as a base for the American Museum of Natural History in the summer of 1957. *Puritan* logged more than 4,000 miles, returning with scientific specimens ranging from mollusks to a whale skull. Bauer was seventy-five years old when *Puritan* was getting ready for her 1961 season. On his trip to the Gulf of California, he suffered a hemorrhage and died a year later. *Puritan* sat at her mooring for two years before a probate court auctioneer sold her to Doyle D. W. Downey.

Downey sailed her to Houston via the Panama Canal and later put her in the charter trade in the Virgin Islands. In 1967 he sold *Puritan* to the son of the Peruvian president, Mariano Prado Sosa. Prado had her delivered to the Merrill-Stevens yard in Miami, where she was refurbished. Her Winston diesel came out and a new GM 8-71 went in. Air-conditioning and a new generator were installed. In Acapulco, the Mexican government seized her on behalf of the Peruvian government, which believed she had been purchased with Peruvian funds. In June 1971 Prado enlisted Bob Fisher of Northrop & Johnson to help him find crew to return *Puritan* to Miami.

After falling into disrepair, she was rescued in 1972 by William Bolling and Gerald Gidwitz of Ft. Lauderdale, who were interested in restoring classic

was a generous and beautifully appointed area with pine paneling (unusual for a yacht) and a beautiful built-in breakfront and cabinetry. She has since been renovated a few times over, but much of the original interior is intact.

Puritan was designed as a topsail schooner; however, she rarely sailed with her tops'ls. One time in the late 1930s she accompanied the TransPac race to Hawaii. She would actually have placed if she had been entered, but due to handicaps given for her size, she did not officially register. In 1941 *Puritan* was sold to the U.S. Navy for one dollar and sent to a navy repair base in San Diego to be re-equipped as a patrol boat for the war effort. Bunks were added on top of bunks, linoleum was put down, and varnish was painted over. She patrolled a two hundred-mile area off the Mexican coast in the vicinity of the Guadeloupe Islands. At one point she had a collision with a ship called *Ramona*, which resulted in breaking off several feet of her bowsprit. When the war was over, Bauer retrieved his yacht and sailed her to Newport Beach for a refit at South Coast Shipyard. There was a complete overhaul and refurbishment,

yachts. They brought her to Riverbend Marina and did a major refit. After 22,000 man-hours, she had new sails, new sheets, new awnings, and tons of new materials! She spent some time in New England and Nova Scotia and even won honors at the Mystic Schooner Race.

Bolling and Gidwitz eventually sold her to Austrian Oskar J. Schmidt. Schmidt had an interest in a hotel on Union Island in the Grenadines and sailed *Puritan* in the Caribbean before taking her for a major refit first in England, then at the Dell'Argentario Yard on the coast of Italy. During an Atlantic crossing in April 1981, she lost her main mast in a horrible storm. Schmidt sailed *Puritan* in the Mediterranean through the late 1980s before selling her to the Feruzzi family who also enjoy her in the Mediterranean. *Puritan* is a one-of-a-kind schooner, and Henry Bauer would be pleased that his beloved yacht is in good condition and in good hands.

The navigation station in the pilothouse aft is a practical, yet comfortable place to escape from the elements.

The dining section is to port with a breakfront opposite the table and a lounge area is to starboard with couches and arm chairs around a coffee table.

The cabins and bathrooms have all been refurbished and slightly altered to accommodate the tastes and needs of the current owners.

Puritan's *original main saloon has remained largely intact. An oddity is that knotty pine was the choice of wood for her interior paneling. Pine was a poor man's wood, and* Puritan *has always been a luxury cruising yacht.*

Type: Ketch
LOA: 71' 11" (21.9 m)
LWL: 63' 10" (19.44 m)
Beam: 16' 1"(4.9 m)
Draft: 7' 9" (2.36 m)
Displacement: 108, 288 lbs.
Hull: Wedge-seamed mahogany,
    carvel planked
Designer: L. Francis Herreshoff
Builder: Legendary Yachts;
    Washougal, Washington
Year built: 1996
Engine: 185 hp Perkins Turbo Diesel

RADIANCE

Radiance is the embodiment of Stan Bishoprick's dream boat. For over thirty years he had wanted to build a replica of Herreshoff's 72-foot ketch, *Ticonderoga*. In the 1950s he and his father had built a 56-foot Herreshoff schooner, out of wood and steel. They laid up the steel frames and stem in Vancouver, then built the rest of the boat on their own property. Father and son flew east to visit L. Francis Herreshoff in Marblehead after they finished the first boat. Bishoprick feels he was probably too young to fully appreciate the meeting. His father, a devotee of Herreshoff, had bound all the *Rudder* magazines from the '40s and '50s because L. Francis at that time was regularly contributing a column called "The Common Sense of Yacht Design," which came out in monthly installments. *Ticonderoga* was Bishoprick's favorite design, so from that time on there was really no other design under consideration. Bishoprick's wife. Nancy, did not grow up sailing, and it was not until she married Stan that she, too, became an enthusiast. *Corahlean*, their first boat, underwent a complete renovation before the Bishoprick family sailed to Hawaii and Alaska. What they loved about *Corahlean* also provided inspiration for *Radiance*.

Radiance was built under a large shed on the same site as the first boat. First Bishoprick, his son, and his son-in-law started lofting up the boat. It subsequently took a crew of ten men 45,000 man hours to complete the boat. Fortunately, Bishoprick was in the construction business and also in the wood pressure-treating business. The boat is built of mahogany and maple from Port Townsend, Washington, and the bronze fittings, port lights, castings, et cetera, were also made in Port Townsend. *Radiance* won Best Sailboat in the Vancouver Boat Show.

Even though *Radiance* is very much a "new classic," the

The newly-built Radiance *was fashioned from L. Francis Herreshoff's design for the 1936 ketch* Ticonderoga. *In 1996, she had the opportunity to compete against both " Ti" and* Whitehawk *in the Opera House Cup Race in Nantucket.*

Nancy's first grandchild. The whole family talks about how solid and stable the boat feels. The interior layout is designed with family cruising in mind—unlike "*Ti*," which was built back in the days of full-time crew, with a forward service galley. *Radiance* enjoys an open plan with galley amidships, open and adjacent to the main saloon. Galley cupboards can be accessed from both sides. There are four spacious double cabins and a special criblike rig on a pilot berth for the baby. *Radiance* is extremely comfortable for living aboard.

Bishoprick has echoed the thoughts of many when he says that wooden boats were not meant to have lasted as long as many of them have. His idea with *Radiance* and her composite structure is to create a yacht of timeless design that will last and last. Still, as *Radiance*, *Ticonderoga*, and *Whitehawk* were racing side by side at the 1996 Opera House Cup Race, sixty-year-old *Ticonderoga* showed no signs of age as compared to her younger sisters.

The interior of Radiance *was custom-designed as a family liveaboard cruiser. To that end, the galley is amidships, open to the main saloon, convenient for family cooking and dining.*

Bishopricks tried to stay with the original *Ticonderoga* design, and they did not want to redesign a new underbody. At 96,000 pounds, she is much lighter than *Ticonderoga* at 110,000. "*Ti*" always enjoyed a reputation for being an extraordinary sailor, and Bishoprick wanted *Radiance* to have the same capability to sail well—and sail she does. She is incredibly balanced. Bishoprick feels that *Radiance* does less pitching than "*Ti*" because she is a little stiffer.

Concessions were made to modern hardware. There is a power winch for hoisting the main; Bishoprick also used new blocks, and because bronze winches were nearly impossible to obtain, he went with stainless-steel self-tailing winches. And similar to *Arawak*, he went with Hall carbon-fiber spars.

Radiance is not only a story of building a dream boat, it is also the story of family togetherness. Bishoprick is now living aboard *Radiance* with his wife, Nancy, his son, Kiel, his daughter, Kelsi, her husband, Will, and their granddaughter, Dori—Stan and

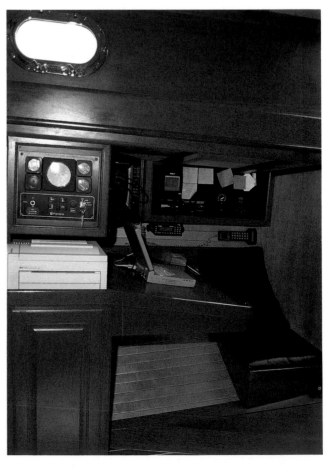

The Bishopricks's granddaughter, Dori, is growing up with true sea legs. Her mother, father and uncle are all helping grandma and grandpa sail Radiance. The boat's first voyage has taken the family from the Pacific Northwest to Mexico, through the Panama Canal to the Caribbean and the East Coast of the U.S.

Type: J Class Boat
LOA: 120' (36.5 m)
LWL: 87' (26.5 m)
Beam: 19' 9" (6 m)
Draft: 15' 6" (4.72 m)
Displacement: 146 U.S. tons
Hull: Teak on steel
Designer: Charles Nicholson
Builder: Camper & Nicholsons;
   Gosport, England
Year built: 1930; restored: 1979 and 1989

SHAMROCK V

hamrock V was the first J Class sloop ever built, one of the only three surviving Js and the only remaining wooden one. Sir Thomas Lipton commissioned *Shamrock V* in 1929–30 from Camper & Nicholsons to pursue his dream of capturing the America's Cup. He had failed four times before—in 1899, 1901, 1903, and 1920. Lipton—a Scotch-Irish sportsman, coffee and tea baron, knight, and gentleman—was anxious to win the cup for his nation and his king. At the age of eighty, he had hoped *Shamrock V* would be the vehicle to achieve his dream. However, he could not beat Harold Vanderbilt's New York Yacht Club defender, *Enterprise*. Much as Vanderbilt was thrilled to have defended the coveted cup, he felt badly for Lipton. He said: "Uppermost in our minds is a feeling of sympathy for that grand old sportsman Sir Thomas Lipton, with whom our relations have been so pleasant." *Shamrock V* went back to England at the end of the 1930 season and Lipton died in 1931.

Shamrock V was lucky to have had a series of devoted owners. Her next owner, British aircraft builder Richard Fairey, improved her underwater shape, rudder configuration, and rig and raced her in the last of the Big Class series of the '30s. She did not race again for fifty years. During World War II, she was purchased by Italian publisher and politician Mario Crespi. He installed her beautiful bird's-eye maple

interior and used her as a cruising boat maintaining her in Bristol condition until the '60s. Sardinian sportsman and businessman, Piero Scanu then acquired her from Crespi and kept her for nearly twenty years in Monte Carlo for day sails and occasional overnight cruises. In the 1970s he and his naval architect son, Paolo, took *Shamrock V* to Camper & Nicholsons for a thorough refit. Unlike *Endeavour* and *Velsheda*, *Shamrock V* has had continuous care throughout her lifetime. In

Her main saloon layout is typical with the dining area to starboard and a settee to port. It is paneled in a striking bird's-eye maple. The tapestry fabrics and Persian rugs create a warm atmosphere below.

1986 the Scanu family sold their beloved boat to the Lipton Tea Company, who, in turn, generously donated her to the Museum of Yachting in Newport, Rhode Island.

In 1989, with help from *Endeavour*'s owner, Elizabeth Meyer, *Shamrock V* had another refit at Newport Offshore. The oversize deckhouse was replaced with a low-profile version, and the high bulwarks were removed and replaced with an original style toe rail. The mast and boom were lengthened and tapered to their original dimensions, and all new standing rigging, running rigging, sails, winches, rudder, steering system, anchoring system, and safety equipment were installed. Belowdecks, new crew quarters and a new galley were created. The berths in all four guest rooms were enlarged, and her fabrics and carpets were changed.

In 1995 *Shamrock V* was purchased by the International Yacht Restoration School in Newport, Rhode Island as part of their classic yacht collection.

Shamrock V is breathtaking under sail; her 87-foot waterline, and towering sail plan—as tall as a sixteen-story building—is as impressive today as it was in 1930.

Eight guests can be luxuriously accommodated in four cabins; one king, one queen, and two twins. The master cabin, pictured here, has Cuban mahogany paneling inlaid with tiger maple.

Type: Ketch
LOA: 112' (34.14 m)
LOD: 100' (30.48 m)
LWL: 93' (28.35 m)
Beam: 22' 6" (6.86 m)
Draft: 8' 5" (2.59 m)
Displacement: 250,000 lbs.
 (113.5 metric tons)
Hull: Mahogany and cedar
Designer: Bruce King
Interior Designer: Joe Artese
Builder: Renaissance Yachts;
 Thomaston, Maine
Year built: 1990
Engine: GMC V-6-92-TA
 (turbo-charged 550 hp)

SIGNE

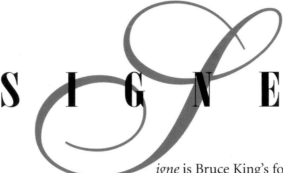

igne is Bruce King's fourth in a series of L. Francis Herreshoff-inspired boats. She has a clipper bow, 15-foot bowsprit and a broad, heart-shaped varnished transom reminiscent of *Ticonderoga*. The Wellmans of Massachusetts who had commissioned *Signe* were enamored of *Whitehawk* and *Whitefin*, two other Bruce King creations, and determined that they would use the same builder, Phil Long of Renaissance Yachts in Thomaston, Maine. Long and King were of the same mind regarding the hull construction. *Signe* was built using the WEST system. Traditional wood was considered and rejected because King believed that it would not have been adequate for *Signe*'s tall rig with high headstay tension. He felt that new classics would all be moving in the direction of cold-molded epoxy. The hull is made up of five layers for a continuous keel-to-deck thickness of 2¾ inches. The interior layer is tongue-and-groove mahogany planking laid fore and aft. Three layers of alternating diagonal epoxied cedar are laid as a core. The sandwich construction is completed by a planked outer mahogany skin. The spars are aluminum because the Wellmans wanted to use the Hood Stoway system. However, they use wooden booms.

Tradition and classic appearance were of primary importance, but it seems as if owner, builder, and

designer were not fanatical in their approach, and modern technology was applied liberally. Joe Artese, formerly of California and currently working out of Washington state, was hired to design the interior space. Artese was largely instrumental in developing polyhedral skylights. He initiated the idea in *Whitehawk* and implemented them in *Whitefin* and *Signe*. The skylight over *Signe*'s main saloon is a decahedron with beveled glass that showers refracted light

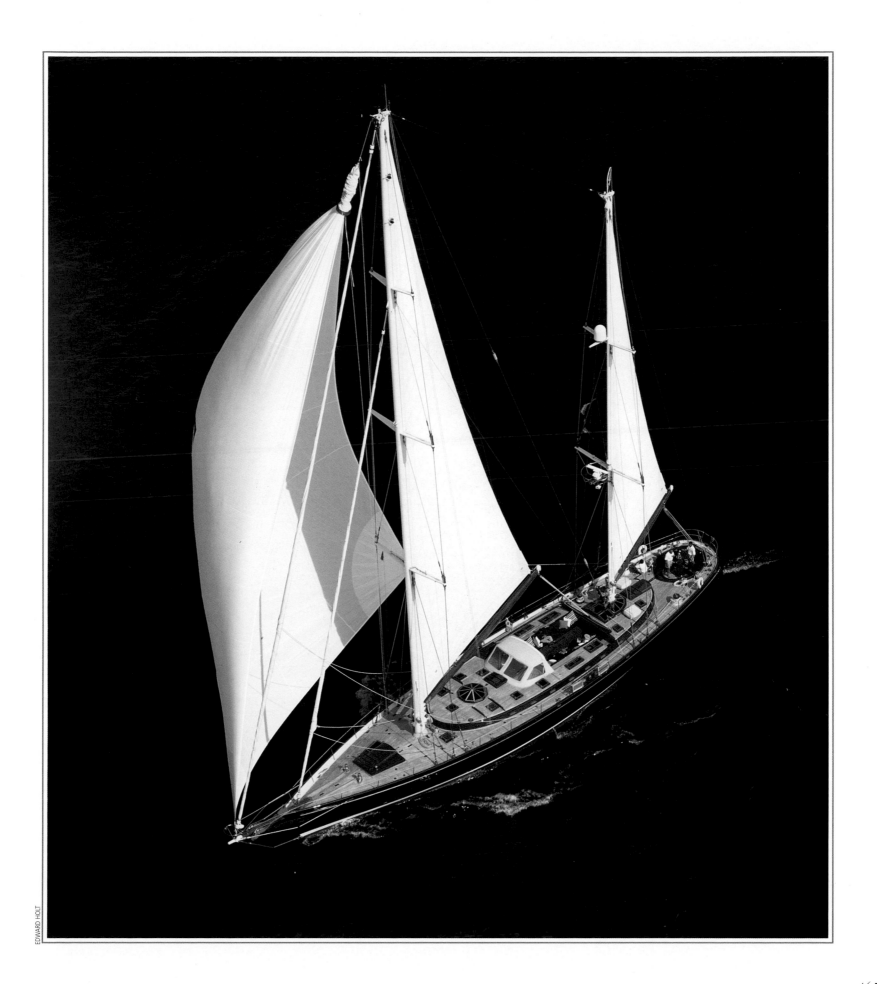

DANA JINKINS

The modern navigation area is to port as you go down the companionway into the main saloon.

The master stateroom has a beautiful curved dresser built into the hull. A nonagon skylight mushrooms from the mizzen mast.

In his design, Bruce King has used exposed structural elements as a way of displaying the boat builder's art, such as the silver-soldered Everdur bronze chainplates in full view in the staterooms, galley, and captain's cabin.

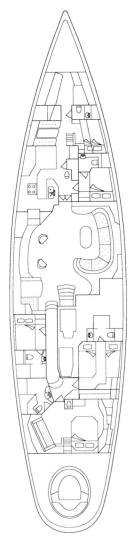

DANA JINKINS

belowdecks. In fact, light is everywhere. There are 17 opening deck hatches, numerous opening ports, and 32 deck lights and prisms. The interior space is exquisite, with curved counters and arched doorways. A rich Hawaiian wood called koa is everywhere. Other wood accents are bird's-eye maple and burled olive wood. A fireplace and built-in semi-circular couch and fine cabinetry add to the elegance of the space. At the entry to the owner's stateroom is a skylight through which the mainmast's permanent backstay passes to join its bronze base. In the owner's stateroom are an off-center double berth and wraparound settees. The skylight, a nonagon, has the mizzenmast actually rising up through it.

The Wellmans named their dream boat after Mary Wellman's late Danish grandmother who lived to be one hundred, and they had hoped to spend their retirement onboard. But unfortunate circumstances led them to sell *Signe* soon after she was launched, and she is now owned by an Englishman who charters her in the Mediterranean.

DANA JINKINS

EDWARD HOLT

EDWARD HOLT

DANA JINKINS

The elegant main saloon is richly textured with a variety of hardwoods—Hawaiian koa, ash, olive burl, and bird's eye maple. A five-foot decagonal skylight of koa and beveled glass crowns the saloon.

The owner's aft cabin stateroom has a queen-size bed and sitting area to starboard.

The en suite bathroom is both elegant and functional with its brass sink and koa-trimmed shower.

Type: Ketch
LOA: 94' (28.9 m)
LWL: 68' (20.8 m)
Beam: 20' (6 m)
Draft: 11' 6" (3.5 m)
Displacement: 130 tons
Hull: Steel
Designer: Laudendorf
Builder: Abeking & Rasmussen;
 Bremen, Germany
Year built: 1959
Engine: 460 hp Caterpillar D343

SINTRA

intra was built in 1959 by Abeking & Rasmussen and designed by Laudendorf. The name "Sintra" is derived from a beautiful village in Portugal, which was the home of many writers and artists. Originally built for a German, *Sintra* was later sold to an Italian, the owner of the Lancia automobile company, who kept her for about six years. Then Martin Thomas, a British yachtsman, scouted her and bought her for a South African gentleman who had her for another seven years. In 1980 an American, Myrna Snider, and her then husband purchased *Sintra* for a transatlantic family adventure. Seventeen years later, the adventure is still going on. Ms. Snider, a lovely high-society Jewish grandmother from Philadelphia, is a most unlikely owner of a yacht. Yet *Sintra* has been her sole residence for the last fifteen years. She tells the story about how when she got divorced, her husband said, "I suppose you want the house." And Myrna replied, "Hell no, you keep the house, I'll take the boat!" Her daughter Tina, who has two small children of her own and often joins her mother for

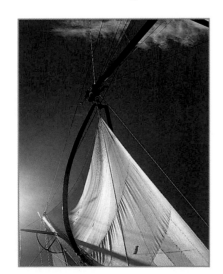

trips, is obviously proud of her. She says, "My mom now files her nails with 220 grit sandpaper and is confident she can get a job varnishing anywhere in the world, if need be." For all four of the grown Snider children, *Sintra* has become "the home they go home to."

The yacht was built for cruising, and with Martin Thomas at the helm for twenty-seven years, she has traveled 120,000 miles around the world. Since *Sintra* is a wishbone ketch, she is easily recognizable whenever she comes into port. Once when Tina was going to meet *Sintra* somewhere on a small island in Greece, her mother could not give her their exact location. Tina said, "Never mind, I'll just look for the wishbone." The concept of a wishbone rig is to create smaller patches of sail area—instead of reefing a sail, you just take it off;

Sintra's *unusual wishbone rig makes her instantly recognizable during a regatta.*

then the combinations of sail you can have up is quite versatile. *Sintra*'s masts are not original—they were remade a little taller in aluminum—and the twin backstays are new as is a mizzen stay, which makes the rig much stronger. Martin Thomas also designed and added the bowsprit to increase the sail area, and he modified the cockpit to have more protection during passages.

Sintra is a classic yacht with the true spirit of a classic. She is always beautifully maintained and maintained with love. She has a full-time crew of five, whom Myrna Snider treats as family. The crew works hard but are also afforded the opportunity to play, as well. When *Sintra* pulls into a new port somewhere in the world, Myrna insists that everyone onboard get off the boat and enjoy the new surroundings and learn about the culture. For Myrna and her family, sailing around the world on *Sintra* has been the best education possible. She says, "You really begin to understand the meaning of 'necessity being the mother of invention' because in the middle of the ocean,

there is no corner hardware store." Myrna Snider is the perfect owner of a classic yacht—her love for her boat and her life are infectious. Many people have said to her, "When are you going to stop this and come back to the real world?" She says, "For me, this *is* the real world!"

The deck saloon is large and airy with an excellent view all around. The dining area is to starboard and the bar and entertainment center are aft and to port.

The pilothouse aft allows the captain a private domain.

The sumptuous owner's cabin is the full width of the boat, with a king-size bed, and built-in desk and cabinetry. The en suite bathroom contains a full size bath, bidet and wash basin.

Type: Schooner
LOA: 82' (24.99 m)
LOD: 70' (21.33 m)
Beam: 16' 10" (5.1 m)
Draft: 11' (3.35 m)
Hull: Teak
Designer: Sparkman & Stephens; New York
Builder: Ah King Slipway; Hong Kong
Year built: 1937; rebuilt 1991–92
Engine: Perkins 125 hp

SO FONG

So Fong is a Sparkman & Stephens topsail schooner with an Asian soul. She was built in 1937 by Ah King Slipway Company in Causeway Bay, Hong Kong, for Thompson Baker, a New York stockbroker. King built quite a few S & S designs. In fact, *So Fong* is a slightly bigger version of the famous Mystic Seaport schooner *Brilliant*.

Apparently because of superstition, the Chinese wouldn't put the boat in the water until she was named. Since no other name was forthcoming, the yard owner chose the nickname for his daughter, which was *So Fong*. The name has remained ever since.

The builder used ironwood for the keelson and floors, her hull is teak, her upper sawn frames are teak and yakkai (a springy Asian wood), and her deck beams are camphor and teak. Her masts and rig were built in the States and shipped to Hong Kong as were her blocks, which are lignum vitae with either bronze or iron straps. Baker commissioned *So Fong* for the purpose of sailing around the world with his son—he did sail her to the U.S. via the East Indies, Suez, Mediterranean, and the Caribbean.

Following his voyage, he sold her.

During the Second World War, she operated as a U.S. Coast Guard vessel, with a seven-man crew. There remains a plaque over the head that says OFFICERS. The skipper had the aft cabin, two officers had the guest cabins, and the four enlisted men were squeezed into the fo'c'sle. After the war *So Fong* spent time in the Caribbean and Maine, under the ownership of Mr. and Mrs. Henry Becton. They raced her, cruised her, refit her, and loved her. But *So Fong* was destined to return to Asia. She was eventually bought by Bill Mathers, who used her as a salvage and diving vessel in the Far East in 1984. In 1986 Mathers was sailing her from Singapore to Hong Kong. *So Fong* was

sixty kilometers off the southwest coast of Vietnam when she was approached and boarded by the Vietnamese militia. The boat was confiscated, and the captain and crew were detained and questioned. Apparently *So Fong*'s high-tech navigation and diving equipment provoked some suspicion. After several months, her two French crew members (and their children) were fined and released. Four months later, the Australian crew was also fined and released. Still under arrest, Mathers was allowed to move back onboard and was told that charges against him would be dropped if he agreed to become a spy. He declined. Nine months after his capture, he was freed after the intervention of the U.S. State Department, and U.N. Secretary General Javier Perez de Cuellar on his behalf. Still, Vietnam retained *So Fong*.

In 1990, Robert Verschoyle, an Irishman of Dutch descent, happened to be in Hai Phong, Vietnam, investigating a potential boatyard site for himself and a partner to start a new business, when he discovered *So Fong*. He negotiated her purchase from the government, and after much red tape and many problems, he sailed her to Saigon and spent the next two years restoring her. Of course, this was no easy feat as there is no such thing as yacht restoration in Vietnam. According to Rob, "There are no shipwrights, just manual laborers—guys who scrubbed or screwed or polished or painted." Rob supervised every step of the way. The team took everything down to the bare hull—the masts came

out, the deck was taken off, and the interior was removed. She was refastened, recoppered, and given a new deck, new rails, and new bulwarks. Her masts are original; she used to be gaff rigged but was changed to Bermudian on the main. The dorades on *So Fong* were made from American 105 Howitzer shells delivered to Vietnam; all her bronze fittings were recast using brass from Howitzer shells. Many of her original fittings had been removed by the Vietnamese and actually ferreted away and buried in people's yards. Through word of mouth, these buried treasures eventually found their way back to *So Fong*.

The refitting of *So Fong* was ultimately an ordeal. Verschoyle credited the Vietnamese with some impeccable workmanship. Still, the frustrations of getting through with the work and actually getting permission to leave were extremely difficult. He finally decided to sneak out of Vietnam. His Vietnamese wife is accused of aiding his escape, and she is no longer allowed to return home.

So Fong, now back from Southeast Asia, is in the Mediterranean and available for charter. Her interior was built with an oriental flair and retains it still.

The doghouse, which is laid out with cushions that can be used as a double bed, is open on the aft end, but can be made private with curtains.

So Fong, *built in Hong Kong, has an Oriental feel. In the main saloon her paneling is camphor wood. A small fireplace on the forward bulkhead is surrounded by tiles painted with Chinese characters.*

Built-in drawers beneath the double bed in the master cabin have carved drawer handles that depict sailing junks and dragons.

The saloon table has carvings on the supports that depict the phoenix battling the dragon. Her fireplace on the forward bulkhead is surrounded by tiles painted with Chinese characters. Her doghouse is separate from the accommodation and totally open from the aft side, providing a unique covered alcove to get out of the elements. This area houses cushions that can be used as a double bed; curtains lend privacy to on deck sleeping. Even this area makes her seem more Asian and exotic!

So Fong has joined the fleet of classics for the series of fall regattas and is proving herself to be quite competitive on the racing circuit.

Type: Schooner
LOA: 115' (35 m)
LOD: 68' (20.72 m)
Beam: 22' 6" (6.85 m)
Draft: centerboard up 5' (1.5 m)
Displacement: 70 tons
Hull: Wood
Builder: Van Cott Shipyard;
  Glen Head, New York
Year built: 1871; rebuilt 1978

STEPHEN TABER

Stephen Taber is the oldest documented sailing vessel in continuous service in the United States today and has been honored by inclusion on the National Historic Register. Launched in 1871, she epitomizes the classic coastal schooner. She cruised New York Harbor before the Brooklyn Bridge was built, and she was present for the first dedication of the Statue of Liberty. Ken and Ellen Barnes, retired theater professors and Coast Guard-licensed co-captains, bought *Stephen Taber* in 1978 and did a major refit on her in Maine. Today, she is run as a very successful Windjammer out of Rockland, Maine. In keeping with her historic nature, there is no inboard power. A yawl boat is relied on for maneuvering in and out of places that require an engine. Originally built on Long Island as a family boat, she was always well maintained. Many coasters were built to last a short time and were ultimately neglected. *Stephen Taber* is a survivor. There is a photo of her from 1880 in Port Jefferson, looking like a yacht, awning set up and all polished—but she was loaded with coal. Obviously she was treated with a great deal of pride. In 1900 her owner, Captain Halleck, had a slow season with cargo. He rigged her up with "ladies' facilities" up forward and chartered her to a wealthy family who followed the New York Yacht Club cruise to Newport. She came to Maine in the 1920s. An honest coaster, she mostly earned her own living in cargo.

In addition to *Stephen Taber*, the Barneses also own a bed and breakfast and *Pauline*. They have a faithful following of repeat guests, some who have sailed with them for ten or fifteen years. *Stephen Taber* is not a luxury yacht, yet she is cozy without being spartan. The main saloon has a tufted-leather settee, a small table, and a wood burning stove. The few small cabins off the saloon have criss-crossing bunks and old-fashioned water pitchers and wash basins. There are only two heads on deck, but that doesn't seem to

The bright, decorative paint job on the anchor windlass and deck pump add character.

There are several wooden barrels that supply water to the galley through a gravity feed from the deck.

The bag-piper, Captain Ken Barnes, entertains guests aboard the Stephen Taber.

be a problem. Most socializing takes place in the galley/dining room. There the cook prepares meals for twenty-two guests on a wood-burning stove. On deck there are several wooden water barrels. The hot water for the galley sink is piped through a coil in the wood stove and is on a gravity feed from the deck barrels. Ken Barnes says it's just like the system in an old farmhouse from the turn of the century. The rustic atmosphere, the hearty food, and the fogged-in harbors on the Maine coast all add up to charm and ambiance aboard *Stephen Taber*.

Most socializing takes place in the galley/dining room. There the cook prepares meals for twenty-two guests on a wood-burning stove.

Stephen Taber *epitomizes the classic coastal schooner. In keeping with her historic nature, there is no inboard power.*

The main cabin with its library and fireplace is small but cozy, especially during those cool Maine evenings.

Type: Ketch
LOA: 120' (36.5 m)
LOD: 105' (32 m)
LWL: 76' (23.16 m)
Beam: 20' (6.09 m)
Draft: 12' 2" (3.71 m)
Displacement: 134.17 tons
Hull: Teak on steel
Designer: Alfred Mylne
Builder: Alexander Stephen & Sons
Restoration: Southampton Yacht Services;
   Southampton, England
Year built: 1937; restored 1994
Engine: 1 x 238 hp Volvo TMD102A diesel

THENDARA

Thendara was special from her very inception. Designed for beauty, speed, and comfort, she was one of the last great racer/cruisers to be commissioned pre-World War II. The golden age of yachting was fading; the economic climate in Britain was becoming increasingly depressed, and yachts of *Thendara*'s ilk were hardly being built any more.

Designed by Alfred Mylne for Scottish MP and inveterate yachtsman Sir Arthur Young, *Thendara* competed regularly against the fleet of yachts of her class (over 60 tons) on the Clyde, on the south coast of England, and at numerous other special regattas. She was quite competitive in her class. At the Torbay Coronation Regatta, following her launching in 1937, she won both first in class and best in overall performance. (She achieved the same honors nearly sixty years later in 1996 at the Cannes Royal Regatta.) At the time she was built, naval architects were shying away from gaff rigs. Nonetheless, Young and Mylne decided to stick with a traditional design. The result is that today, *Thendara* is one of the most

distinctive classic ketches under sail. Often during a classic yacht regatta, it is difficult for the uninitiated to recognize which yacht is which. With *Thendara*'s large jackyard topsails there is no confusion. Her rig sets her apart from all others.

During the war, *Thendara* ceased her racing career and was conscripted in the British navy as a barrage balloon boat. She suffered some misuse and damage during these years, for which Sir Arthur was later compensated. Postwar, *Thendara* had her stem replaced as well as several planks. Although competitive large boat racing had all but ceased, Sir Arthur continued to cruise *Thendara*. He died aboard the yacht in 1950 at one of his favorite anchorages at Benodet in Brittany.

Thendara was sold and ended up in Greece for a number of years.

The chart table extension which pulls out from the port side cupboard forward of the settee is cleverly concealed when not in use.

Her original rig was changed to Marconi during this time. From 1986–89, when she was under Australian ownership, *Thendara* was at the Cantieri Navali Valdetarro at La Spezia, undergoing an extensive refit. Still, the most extensive and thorough refit took place at Southampton Yacht Services starting in 1991, after a change in ownership. *Thendara* had finally found an owner like her original one, someone in love with classic yachts who was determined to restore her to her full glory.

No doubt *Altair* had set a precedent at Southampton Yacht Services for the restoration of *Thendara*. Her renovation was undertaken with serious attention to detail by Mike Horsley, the project manager. Original drawings and photographs were procured, and three designers set about their tasks: Edwin Meayers supervised the interior, Midship Boat Services handled the engineering and structural arrangements, and Alan Boswell produced the external drawings. What occurred was a rebirth! Starting from the remarkably intact steel skeleton of the yacht, new floor bearers, tanks, and bearers for the modernized engine room were fitted out. *Thendara* was refitted totally and completely. New decks of marine plywood were scarfed and glued into a watertight layer and overlaid by one-inch teak bedded on an epoxy-resin mixture. Bulwarks were framed and fitted to fair with existing pieces. Along with a new transom and a new laminated stem, four top teak planks were replaced. A new Iroko rudder was fabricated according to original plans. All sorts of fittings such as cleats, eye-bolts, stanchions, and bronze fair leads were either refurbished or replaced. Hatches, skylights, and dorade boxes were rebuilt in the style of the original items. Preserving the historical integrity of all facets was of paramount importance.

The deck is vast, expansive, and beautiful. The skylights and vents added for the comfort of down below don't detract from the deck's clean lines. There is a knee-deep cockpit aft of the doghouse for comfortable seating under way or at anchor. Additionally, there is a dining table on deck forward of the doghouse. The helmsman stands in the traditional position aft to steer the boat. In front of the steering pedestal is a 1930s carved compass binnacle. All gauges and instrumentation are handily hidden under a flap when not in use.

Since *Thendara* arrived at Southampton Yacht Services with no masts and no original interior, they had to be recreated. Harry Spencer replicated her rig from old drawings and photographs. Her spars are Colombian pine and spruce. There are no aluminum or stainless-steel rigging wires. Her sails are the obligatory cream-colored variety from Ratsey & Lapthorn. Her doghouse, was lowered to create a more pleasing profile. It is paneled in teak, and the facing settees double as pilot berths complete with lee cloths. A clever concealed chart table pulls out from the port-side cupboard just forward of the settee.

The main saloon has been recreated with the classically configured U-shaped dining section opposite a settee lounge area. Part of the interior is painted an eggshell color and the rest is paneled in Honduran mahogany. Period fixtures have been obtained to retain the '30s feel of the yacht.

Her interior has been thoughtfully designed in the original style. Honduran mahogany paneling and eggshell paint grace the entire belowdecks. The main saloon is classically configured with a U-shaped dining area opposite a settee lounge area. The upholstery is a regal red-and blue-stripe. A lot of light is emitted through a large skylight. Simplicity reigns in the master stateroom and the guest cabins. Period fixtures have been obtained to retain the '30s feel of the yacht. *Thendara* is another successful restoration by Southampton Yacht Services, who are to be commended for their excellence in capturing the essence of a bygone era.

Type: Ketch
LOA: 85' (25.9 m)
LOD: 72' (21.94 m)
LWL: 68' 9" (20.95 m)
Beam: 16' (4.88 m)
Draft: 7' 10" (2.4 m)
Displacement: 119, 016 lb.
Hull: Double-planked mahogany
Designer: L. Francis Herreshoff
Builder: Quincy Adams Yacht Yard;
  Quincy, Massachusetts
Year built: 1936; restored; 1989
Engine: GMC 130 hp

TICONDEROGA

*T*iconderoga is probably one of the most famous names in American yachting. When she retired from truly competitive racing at the age of thirty one, she held more than thirty elapsed time records for mostly major events. In 1996 she celebrated her sixtieth birthday. Jack Somer, who has written a lively, comprehensive history of this yacht, entitled *Ticonderoga, Tales of an Enchanted Yacht*, attributes her inception to Waldo Hayward Brown who collaborated with L. Francis Herreshoff to build a 50-foot schooner, *Joanna*, in 1923. Brown came to Herreshoff with an oil painting of his grandfather's clipper-bow pilot boat built in Salem, Massachusetts, in 1850. Then he ordered a 57-foot ketch called *Tioga*. Harry Noyes bought *Tioga* from Brown but soon determined that he wanted a larger vessel.

He asked Herreshoff to design a scaled-up version of *Tioga*. Noyes owned the Quincy Adams Yacht Yard and built his new Herreshoff there. Herreshoff claims that Noyes really wanted a comfortable day sailer. Noyes had a mind of his own and kept changing it. The designer/builder relationship was not easy. Bad blood developed between the two, primarily over money but also over methods and decisions. A designer generally gets 10–15 percent of the builder's fee, and Herreshoff felt that Noyes, as owner/builder, was undercutting the building costs, thus shaving Herreshoff's fee. Also, Noyes was a will-

ful owner and didn't take suggestions well, such as where to purchase the sails. Herreshoff wanted to commission them from Ratsey in New York, but Noyes wanted to get them from England. And so it went. The launching in 1936 was a wild event. The cradle poppets gave way, and the huge hull slid off the rails as the cradle collapsed. *Tioga* amazingly did not sustain significant damage.

In 1940 Noyes died in a plane crash. His wife and family

PATRICIA LASCABANNES

Ticonderoga, *heeled over and racing for the mark at Antigua Classic Yacht Regatta.*

her hauled and did a lot of structural work on her at the Miami Shipyard. Later he did more work at Minneford's in New York. Hertz raced her in numerous races, though he had a reputation for being difficult, particularly with his hired skippers. In 1960 Baxter Still and Bill Brittain teamed up to buy *"Ti"* for $65,000. They sailed her to the Caribbean and through the Panama Canal. In 1961 she did her first Transpacific Race. She clocked many miles with those owners, often winning or placing in major regattas. In 1962 she went back east for the America's Cup, and in 1963 she did the SORC, racing from St. Petersburg to Ft. Lauderdale and Miami to

did not have the spirit to sail *Tioga*, so they put her up in a shed. In 1942 Ruth Noyes lent her to the U.S. Coast Guard for war service. Her hull was painted a battleship gray, and she was used to patrol the East Coast. She was given back to Ruth Noyes after the war, along with $11,000 to help cover some of the wear and tear. Allan Carlisle found her in the Quincy Adams yard in 1946 and bought her from the estate. Since Ruth Noyes wanted to retain the name *Tioga* out of sentimentality, Carlisle came up with another old Indian word, *Ticonderoga*, now the name of a village and eighteenth-century fort on Lake Champlain.

Carlisle did a lot of race charters to help pay the bills. He had the spars rebuilt at the A. E. Luders Yard in Stamford, Connecticut. In 1951 Carlisle ended up selling her for financial reasons. John Hertz Jr., son of the founder of Hertz rental cars, bought her through Dick Bertram, who had sailed with Carlisle. Hertz had

Montego Bay. In 1963 Bob Johnson chartered her for the TransPac. Baxter Still had a problem with letting Johnson take his own crew, even though the boat was chartered to him. The difficulties between them were resolved when Johnson purchased *Ticonderoga*. Johnson struck up a friendship with Herreshoff and had a long correspondence with him, asking his advice before a refit in Newport Beach.

Probably the last of *Ticonderoga*'s major ocean racing took place in 1966—a new breed of plastic, composite, and metal boats were on the scene. *"Big Ti"* sailed extensively, but by then Johnson was devoting his energy to his new boat, *Windward Passage.* He tried to donate *"Ti"* to the Mystic Seaport Museum, but they couldn't afford her, so he donated her to Nova University in Ft. Lauderdale. She had been stripped of so much of her gear by the people building *Windward Passage* that she needed her own per-

One of the most famous boats in American yachting, Ticonderoga is magnificent and extremely fast under sail. At one time, she held thirty elapsed-time records for major racing events. Today she is still quite competitive and active in the classic yacht regattas.

Ticonderoga has three cabins. The master cabin has a large double bunk with en suite head. The two guest cabins have pullman upper and lower bunks with a shared head. The plaid wool blankets are a testimony to her New England heritage.

sonal refit. In 1967 Nova University sold *"Ti"* to Robodor Corporation, which was owned by Robert S. Robe from Oyster Bay, New York. He paid only $30,000 for her but put $100,000 into her at Spencer's yard so that he could charter her. She was then purchased by Englishman Brian Coen for $75,000. He loved her and chartered her in the Caribbean but was prevailed upon to sell her to Ken MacKenzie in the early '70s for a price double what he had paid. MacKenzie and his wife, Fran, ran *"Ti"* as a charter boat in New England and the Caribbean for ten years. They cruised her, raced her, and took great pride in ownership. But they ran her on their proceeds from charter, and sometimes the charter season was not very good. Rolex hired her for a commercial in 1975–76, which helped a bit, but the MacKenzies ended up selling her in 1981 to David Edwards, who also used her for charter.

Her next owner was Bob Voit, who pumped nearly one million dollars into her. Voit commissioned a world-class restoration at Southampton Yacht Services in 1988–89, hiring John Munford to revamp the interior. With his skipper, Tom Reardon, Voit sailed her extensively in the States, the Caribbean and in Europe. In 1993 the current owner, Scott Frantz, heard that she was for sale and was determined to fulfill his lifetime dream of owning her. When Frantz was a boy, his father had owned *Sorrento*, and he had often come in contact with *Ticonderoga* and always admired her. Tom Reardon is still the skipper on board. *Ticonderoga* is in the best of all possible hands. Frantz and his wife, Icy, know what a special yacht they have. They enjoy her with family and friends, sail her in classic yacht regattas, and maintain her in the pristine condition that she deserves.

Ticonderoga's *main saloon was redesigned by
John Munford and constructed at Southampton
Yacht Services during her extensive restoration
in 1988–89. She has a lounge area to starboard
and dining table to port.*

Type: Sloop
LOA: 92' (28 m)
LOD: 74' (22.7 m)
LWL: 49' (15.2 m)
Beam: 14' (4.3 m)
Draft: 10' (3.0 m)
Hull: Semi composite steel and steamed frames
Designer: William Fife
Builder: William Fife & Sons;
   Fairlie, Scotland
Restoration: Fairlie Restorations; Hamble, U.K.
Year built: 1909, restored 1993
Engine: 84 hp 4JH2DTE Yanmar

TUIGA

uiga is one of the finest remaining examples of the early 15 meter class designed by William Fife. Built in 1909 at Fairlie in Scotland for the Duke of Medinacelli, close friend of King Alphonse XIII—the two shared a passion for sailing. King Alphonse owned her sister ship, *Hispania*, and possibly *Tuiga* was conceived as a competitor to the king's yacht. Construction took only eight months, and shortly after her launching she was delivered to Santander in Spain by a British crew to participate in a series of races. Her racing career spanned many years—for some reason, perhaps diplomatic, she never beat *Hispania* but often finished a close second.

Between World War I and World War II, *Tuiga* frequently changed hands—and names: *Betty IV*, *Dorina*, *Kismet III*, and *Nevada*. After the second war, a young couple bought her, restored her name, and attempted to get her back on track; unfortunately they fell on hard times, and *Tuiga* ended up in Cyprus in a very run-down state. Her next owner organized a rough refit to sail her back to England. Still, *Tuiga* was suffering from old age and lack of care—it was not surprising that she took on a lot of water. Her crew considered abandoning her but managed to persevere to her destination.

Tuiga started life with royal affiliations, so it is fitting that she is now the flagship of the Yacht Club

NICOLAS CLERC

of Monaco and ambassador to the principality. *Tuiga* is a fairly faithful restoration without many of the modern conveniences of new technology. (The yacht club likes the idea of teaching young sailors what it was really like to sail in the days before electronics and even winches.) Her construction, typical of the meter boats of her period before the Second World War is semicomposite wood with steel frames alternating with steamed. The deck is yellow pine laid over plywood substructure. The deck structures are Brazilian mahogany as are the planks and covering board. The bronze fastenings have

been electrically insulated from the steel to minimize any potential electrolysis. Nickel aluminum bronze and cast replicas of the original deck fittings further enhance the "look" of the boat. A new rig was constructed after thorough research to replicate the original. The spars are Colombian pine; the lower mast and bowsprit are solid, the rest are hollow. The mast fittings are all in the original style. The sail wardrobe, which consists of eight sails, are of the finest quality and workmanship. The lower sails are hand stitched from narrow-paneled cloth dyed the color of the original Egyptian cotton.

Her accommodation is fairly original; the owner's cabin has twin berths, the furniture is off-white-painted tulip wood trimmed with varnished mahogany. To port aft is a guest shower; forward of it is a guest head to starboard and a single cabin to port. The main saloon is a full-width room with mahogany paneling to waist height and a lighter wood above. Forward are the galley and crew's quarters. Throughout, mahogany-paneled cupboards and cabinets are used for storage and to hide electrical panels and the switchboard.

Tuiga can be seen, often with Prince Albert at the helm, on the classic yacht regatta circuit at all the major events from Porto Cervo and Livorno, to Cannes and the Nioulargue in St. Tropez, to Palma and elsewhere. Under sail she is regal, indeed!

T U I G A

Although the galley is probably seldom used these days, it is well-organized with plenty of counter space.

The owner's cabin has twin berths with settees alongside each. The tulip wood furniture is painted an off white and trimmed with varnished mahogany.

The main saloon walls are distinctive, in that the mahogany paneling is waist-height with a lighter wood trimmed in mahogany above. Nowhere on Tuiga is there evidence of the modern technology or the 1990s.

Type: Gaff-headed sloop
LOA: 52' (15.84 m)
Beam: 14' (4.26 m)
Draft: 5' 6" (1.67 m)
Displacement: Approximately 45,000 lbs.
Hull: Planked cedar on oak frames
Designer: Havilah Hawkins
Builder: Nigel Bower and Mike Geer,
  Wooden Boat Co.; Camden, Maine
Year built: 1996

VELA

ela is the inspiration of Havilah "Haddie" Hawkins. Haddie's father Havilah "Bud" Hawkins designed, built, skippered, and sailed boats his whole life. Young Haddie likes to say he was born on the *Stephen Taber* and grew up crewing on his father's 83-foot Maine windjammer, *Mary Day.* There was never a question as to what his future would involve. Launched in late spring 1996, *Vela* is a gaff-rigged sloop, essentially double-ended from the keel almost up to the waterline. She looks like a hybrid—a cross between an English fishing boat and a Maine coaster, with some Alden and Herreshoff thrown in. *Vela* was built by Haddie and Nigel "Twig" Bower at Bower's Wooden Boat Construction shop in Camden, Maine. Haddie has been drawing boats for years but never had formal training. The frames are sawn white oak, and the planking is cedar. Haddie believes in simplicity. He says he is tired of schooners where "there're two of everything: two masts, two booms, two gaffs, two, two, two…too many bits of string." He says he is not made of money, and a gaff sloop is just perfect for him. There are no overhangs, no bowsprit, and the wide deck is uncluttered. He does have a single headsail and a very large mainsail, 800 square feet on a 35-foot boom. He says, "Topping lifts and lazy jacks make sailing easy; when you drop the sail, gravity enables it to fold automatically." He calls his

boat a work boat. He was keen on proving a point that you don't need to be a millionaire; that anyone of modest means can build a good, solid, efficient boat. To that end he was fortunate to have been able to purchase a lot of equipment and fittings from *Arawak* (the former *Christmas*). Hawkins was adamant that no time be spent searching for the perfect lumber—that his boat be built from "off-the-shelf stock."

The sawn frames were made of scarfed-together pieces to produce the required curves. It took just ten weeks to pour the lead-bal-

last keel, make and set up all the frames and the backbone, build the transom, and fit the deck beams. There is no varnish on the boat, just pine tar. Hawkins thinks you should build a boat that has the kind of maintenance you enjoy doing—and he loves the smell of pine tar. The interior layout is open and rustic, of hardware-store pine. A large cargo hatch over the main saloon lets in a lot of light when open. Eventually they will have a tarp over the area and keep the hatch open in fine weather. There are no bulkheads to speak of, the master bed is athwarships aft, and two children's bunks are port and starboard. This is a family liveaboard boat. Charters are limited to day trips out of Edgartown on Martha's Vineyard. The Hawkins children, Mari and Caleb, are following in their father's and grandfather's footsteps—growing up on and around boats. Haddie and Beverly Hawkins enjoy children and have a dream of stopping in cities like Boston and Philadelphia on their way south some year in order to introduce inner city kids to sailing. *Vela* is Hawkins's dream boat—he says he had to build her to get it out of his system.

Haddie Hawkins, owner and builder of Vela, *calls his vessel a work boat; a hybrid between an English fishing boat and a Maine coaster. He designed her to be easy to sail with his young family.*

The Hawkins children, Mari and Caleb, are following in their father's and grandfather's footsteps—they are growing up on, and around boats.

The interior layout is open and rustic, built of "hardware-store pine". There are no bulkheads, the master bed is forward athwartships with a handy companionway up to the cockpit. The two children's bunks are port and starboard. Functional and spare as it is, belowdecks exudes comfort and charm.

A large cargo hatch over the main saloon is always open in fine weather.

Type: Ketch
LOA: 45' 8" (13.9 m)
Beam: 13' 6" (4.11 m)
Draft: 6' (1.83 m)
Displacement:24 tons
Hull: Larch, yellow pine, oak
Builder: James Noble Yard;
  Fraserburgh, Scotland
Year built: 1911, Restored; 1987–91
Engine: Ford 80 hp Diesel

VIOLET

Violet, a Scots Zulu, was built in 1911 at the James Noble Yard in Fraserburgh, Scotland, for Alex Stephen. The Zulu class was a combination of two traditional Scottish vessels, the Fifie and the Scafie. The name "Zulu" was derived from the British-Zulu war, which was waged around 1880. As the concept of the Zulu was to improve the safety of the Scottish fishing fleet, it is anyone's guess why that name was chosen. *Violet* is a little smaller than the traditional Zulu but nonetheless typical of her class. The rig of these vessels was designed to allow them to outperform any other working boat in the British Isles. Two loose-footed lug sails were set on enormous unstayed masts, and a jib was set on a long reefing bowsprit offset to port. The yard was hoisted on the lee side of the mast. The effect was beautiful and efficient to a point—the drawback being that the sail had to be lowered to the deck and carried around to the new lee side at every tack!

Under Stephen's ownership, *Violet* worked at driftnetting for herring and small-line fishing in the off-season. She was given an auxiliary engine in the '20s but maintained her sailing rig until 1936.

When Stephens retired, his son John converted *Violet* to power and with the help of his brothers continued to fish her for forty more years. In 1975 *Violet* was sold to Carleton Sprague of Vineyard Haven, Massachusetts. She was renamed *John B. Manning,* and Sprague used her for fishing out of Cork, Ireland, for two years. In 1977 Bob Douglas of Martha's Vineyard and *Shenandoah* fame purchased her and towed her all the way to Vineyard Haven. Douglas intended to refit her and use her as a work boat; however, she languished, neglected first on a mooring in Vineyard Haven Harbor, then sitting derelict on a railway by the Black Dog Tavern until Gary Maynard rescued her in 1987.

Since the original "Zulus" had their share of peculiarities, Gary Maynard
re-rigged Violet to suit his needs for sailing comfortably with his family.
He can hoist the 570-square-foot mainsail himself and the topsail, jib,
and mizzen can all be easily handled with the help of his wife Kristi.

The main saloon and galley are functional, and at the same time cozy and colorful. The hand-painted tiles depict scenes of the family and friends who helped with the renovation.

Violet had now changed hands for the fourth time since she was launched. Maynard—who had sailed around the world with his family aboard their *Spray* replica, *Scud*, worked as the galley boy on the traditional topsail schooner *Shenandoah* and aboard several other vessels as bosun, mate, captain, rigger, and carpenter—was well qualified for the task at hand. Maynard had the passion, enthusiasm, and talent to resurrect a well-worn classic. He made an arrangement to purchase *Violet* from Bob Douglas for $6,000 if Douglas would provide space in his shed so that Maynard could rebuild her.

Maynard and his then girlfriend—now wife—Kristi Kinsman devoted four years to the labor-intensive project of restoration. They began by tearing out everything that might have needed replacing such as her fo'c'sle bunks, fish pens, engine room, and concrete in the bilges. Next came her decking, rail caps, stanchions, hatch coamings, guards, and even her sheer strakes and garboards. Work on the frames took three months because it turned out that most of the thirty-two frames on each side had to be replaced top to bottom. Next, the planking was either replaced or sistered where salvageable. When possible, Maynard used the old nailheads. Cohort Kinsman painstakingly picked out the old putty and rust and cleaned and filled the old nails with epoxy paint and thickened epoxy after applying Ospho.

After frames and planking, they had to determine the deck configuration, placement of deck-houses, cockpit, and the like. Aesthetics as well as practicality were reasoned with careful consideration. Six seemed to be a magic number: the boat was purchased for $6,000, approximately 6,000 hours of personal labor went into her, and about $60,000 was spent for materials, most of which was earned by Maynard and Kinsman during the hours they were not actually working on *Violet*.

According to Gary Maynard, consistency and aesthetics play a key role in restoring a boat like *Violet*. In a detailed article that Maynard wrote for *Wooden Boat* Magazine, he set up the following guidelines: 1) Be consistent with the scale of all the various parts. 2) Be consistent with the period of the vessel—keep the technology and materials in the realm of the possible for the age of the boat. For instance, maintain cast bronze or galvanized as opposed to stainless steel on a traditional boat. 3) Keep things simple, crisp, clean, be spare with the router—and let the curves of the vessel speak for themselves. 4) Keep the level of finish work consistent; avoid tool marks or chatter marks from the planer. 5) Be judicious in wood choices, making sure they blend well together. 6) Remember that everything you do can be a statement of beauty and utility.

The interior of *Violet* is cozy and friendly. The hand-painted tiles depicting family and friends are definitely a focal point in the main saloon. All the interior joinery is of simple, modest construction. There is mostly painted white pine with eight coats of hand-rubbed mahogany trim. She is a lovely boat through and through. Maynard is a purist when it comes to wooden boat restoration. He likes to point out that *Violet* is so accessible because she is, after all, made from sticks of wood, bolts, rope, and a little sail cloth.

Violet's interior paneling is mostly painted white pine with mahogany trim. Since the Maynards spend a lot of time aboard the boat with their two small children, their personal touches create their own special aesthetic.

Baby Clara is delighted with her very own bunk which is rigged with a beautiful lace safety net for security at sea.

Type: Schooner
LOA: 80' (24.38 m)
LOD: 63' 6" (19.35 m)
LWL: 47' (14.33 m)
Beam: 15' (4.57 m)
Draft: 9' (2.74 m)
Displacement: 43 tons
Hull: Cedar and mahogany
Designer: John G. Alden
Builder: F. F. Pendleton; Wiscasset, Maine
Restoration: Gannon & Benjamin Boatyard;
    Martha's Vineyard, Massachussetts
Year built: 1938; rebuilt 1991–94
Engine: GM 4-71 Diesel

WHEN AND IF

When and If was designed by John Alden in 1938 and built by F. F. Pendleton in Wiscasset, Maine, for George S. Patton. A heavily built schooner, her hull was double planked with mahogany over cedar. At the time of the commission, Patton was a U.S. Army colonel with a vision of sailing his boat around the world, "*when* the next war is over, and *if* I live through it." The tumult in Europe and the uncertainty of his own future is reflected in a letter he wrote to Clifford Swaine (the man who drew *When and If*'s lines), confiding that (quoting Swaine) "he was passed over twice for promotion to brigadier general by President Roosevelt and that if, as anticipated, he were passed over a third time, he would resign from the army and cruise in his new boat around Cape Horn to the West Coast and Catalina Island, which his family once owned." War broke out, and Patton, of course, played a major role leading the Allied forces overseas. He never had the opportunity to fulfill his dream; though he survived the war, he was killed in an automobile accident in Europe in 1945.

When and If remained in Patton's family until 1972. His wife, Beatrice Ayer Patton, passed the boat to her brother, Frederick Ayer, who in turn passed her on to Frederick Ayer Jr. All this time, her home port had remained Manchester Harbor, Massachusetts. Ayer Jr. donated her to the Landmark School for Dyslexic Children in Beverly, Massachusetts. The school created a semester at sea program around *When*

and If. Because of financial problems at the school, director Charlie Harris, entered into an unusual arrangement with publisher and yachting enthusiast Jim Mairs and his wife, Gina: The boat was to be shared by both parties. The agreement was reached, a contract was signed, but a few weeks prior to the closing date, a fierce gale forced *When and If* to break loose from her mooring and go up on the rocks in Manchester.

After a salvage crew brought her to their yard in Salem, it was obvious that she had been badly damaged. There was a huge gaping hole in her port side, broken frames, twisted cabin sole, thoroughly demolished interior, destroyed rudder, smashed keel—problems galore. Seven boatyards were approached to bid on her restoration. The project was beginning to look infeasible. Daunted by the magnitude of the undertaking required to restore *When and If*, Mairs called Ross Gannon of Gannon and Benjamin Boatyard in Martha's Vineyard to see if there were any possible solutions short of giving up. Gannon and Benjamin suggested becoming partners in the boat and working out an equitable arrangement with the Landmark School. The restoration was a long, careful process that lasted for three years.

Two-thirds of the planking on the port side was replaced as were parts of the deck, the rudder, and the propeller. The boat had held up remarkably well for being over a half-century old. There was no rot or metal damage. Some of the sawn oak frames were replaced with locust, and bronze was a major theme: bronze fastenings, bronze floors, and cast bronze hanging knees, everything strapped in bronze.

She is a very heavily built boat. At 43 tons, she has been accused of being overbuilt and overrigged. Like most boats, she loves a reach; sailing on her there is a real sense of security. The masts are original, and the aft cabin is original, but forward is new. She deserved a new configuration because she was no longer a school boat. The wood paneling is cypress from an old water tank, while yellow pine and other used wood, complete with distress marks, makes the interior look old. The systems are all new, including a hot-water shower. Jim Mairs, Nat Benjamin, and Ross Gannon could all be accused of being hopeless romantics, but if it weren't for them, *When and If* would be only a memory.

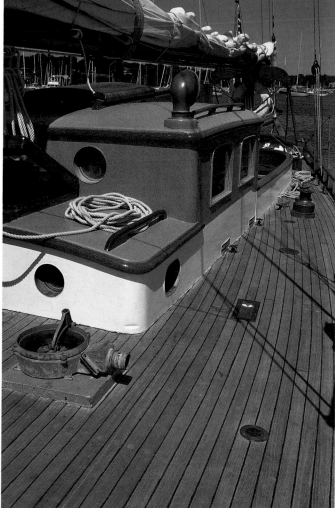

Her main saloon and forward section are new, however the cypress paneling is from an old water tank, and the yellow pine and mahogany, complete with distress marks make the interior look old. The feeling belowdecks is warm and comfortable—not at all fussy.

The main saloon has two single berths, one port and one starboard. There are three private cabins, each with double berths.

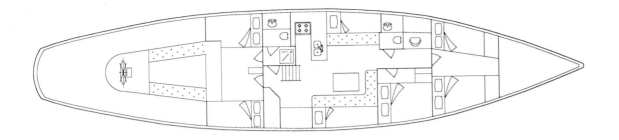

The galley is well equipped and secure for the cook with its U-shaped configuration. The storage spaces are open and easy to get to. Everything about When and If *is functional and thoughtfully conceived.*

Type: Ketch
LOA: 105' (32 m)
LOD: 92' (28 m)
LWL: 78' 6" (23.93 m)
Beam: 20' 6" (6.25 m)
Draft: centerboard up 7' 5" (2.29 m)
Draft: centerboard down 16' 10" (5.12 m)
Displacement: 90 tons
Hull: Cold-molded wood (WEST system)
Designer: Bruce King
Builder: O. Lie-Nielson; Rockland, Maine
Year built: 1978

WHITEHAWK

Whitehawk, the 92-foot stretch version of the famous sixty-year-old L. Francis Herreshoff ketch, *Ticonderoga*, was built by O. Lie-Nielson at Lee's Boat Shop in Rockland, Maine, in 1978. She was the brainchild of Californian Phil Long, who conceived her as an ocean racer capable of beating *Flying Cloud*'s record run between New York and San Francisco..

In the early '70s, Long came to Maine to buy *Bounty*, a smaller version of *Ticonderoga*. One thing led to another, and Long decided he really wanted a larger boat—much larger. Using *Ticonderoga*'s design as a point of departure, naval architect Bruce King was called in to apply the advances of modern technology to the design. *Whitehawk* was to be a masterpiece of character, craftsmanship, and engineering. One day renowned artist Andrew Wyeth walked into Lee's Boat Shop and marveled at *Whitehawk*, saying she was as much a masterpiece as any painting in a museum.

Whitehawk's hull is the WEST system, made of thin wooden strips—four layers of cedar and one of mahogany, glued together and bonded in epoxy. She was one of the largest boats to have this cold-molded technique. The result is a strong but light hull. While she is not exactly a wooden boat, she employs a lot of Alaskan cedar, Maine cedar, Burmese teak, white oak from Appalachia, yellow pine from Georgia, and sitka spruce from Oregon. She has a traditional design with sweeping, expansive teak decks, varnished deckhouses and trim, and a generous curved cockpit. Her interior boasts a 21-foot

main saloon with fireplace. She has two commodious guest cabins with en suite bathrooms and a magnificent master stateroom with a laminated wood bathtub. Her sheer gives her an incomparable profile, and her huge raked masts are recognizable in any harbor. The main mast is 116-feet tall carrying 4,484 square feet of sail. However, the potential sail area is 13,000 square feet which allows *Whitehawk*

WHITEHAWK

to reach speeds under sail as high as 16 knots.

Although Long spent three years building the boat for himself, he decided to sell her to Thomas Zetkov right after her launching. Zetkov enjoyed *Whitehawk* for many years, cruising, racing, and chartering her primarily in New England. In 1986 *Whitehawk* had a frightening accident in the narrow Cape Cod Canal. Captain Steve Smalec, enroute to a classic yacht regatta in Newport, Rhode Island, had a collision with a 641-foot freighter. There was pea soup fog, and Smalec had been tracking the freighter on his radar when *Whitehawk*'s two masts hit a steel overhang on the freighter's bow and were snapped off at their base. The hull was undamaged, the crew was not injured, and the masts were eventually replaced.

In 1990 John and Heather Dwight of Vermont purchased *Whitehawk* and have continually poured love and money into keeping her pristine. They restored the crew's quarters, renovated her interior, created an additional guest cabin and revamped the main saloon. They have made her the epitome of a racer/cruiser. The Dwights sail on her in New England and the Mediterranean in the summers and in the Caribbean in the winters with family and friends. They also like to enter *Whitehawk* in the classic yacht regattas in Antigua, Maine, Nantucket, and Newport. In the summer of 1996 *Whitehawk* had the opportunity to compete against her "cousins,"

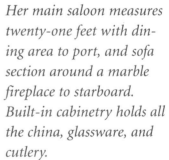

Her main saloon measures twenty-one feet with dining area to port, and sofa section around a marble fireplace to starboard. Built-in cabinetry holds all the china, glassware, and cutlery.

The master cabin features a queen-size bed and a beautiful large laminated wood bathtub.

WHITEHAWK

Ticonderoga and newcomer *Radiance*, at the Opera House Race in Nantucket.

In the fall of 1996, enroute to the Caribbean via Bermuda, *Whitehawk* had another tragedy. She was anchored off St. George's Island when captain Jim Murphy noticed smoke coming out of the engine room. While the crew fought to contain the fire, she was towed to a dock where it took the Bermuda Fire Brigade five hours to fully extinguish the fire. In the process, holes were cut in the teak decks with a chain saw to gain access. A week following the fire, the boat was towed back to Rhode Island to have work done at Little Harbor Marina. While there was no damage to the hull, the main engine, generators, electronics, hydraulics, and all the electrical wiring had to be totally replaced. She required new refrigerators and freezers and the aft section of the galley had to be rebuilt. The base of the mizzenmast was repaired and over twenty-seven feet of teak deck replaced.

With the work having been completed in the summer of 1997, *Whitehawk* is off sailing looking as elegant as ever.

Type: Yawl
LOA: 73' 3" (22.36 m)
LWL: 52' 6" (16 m)
Beam: 15' 5" (4.70 m)
Draft: 9' 6" (2.90 m)
Displacement: 50 tons
Hull: Mahogany
Designer: Sparkman & Stephens; New York
Builder: Henry R. Hinckley Co.;
  Southwest Harbor, Maine
Year built:1956; refitted 1987
Engine: Perkins 130 hp diesel

W I N D I G O

indigo, some may argue, is a production boat, and therefore, she cannot be construed as a classic. However, the 73-foot yawl, designed by Sparkman & Stephens and built by the Henry Hinckley Company in 1956 certainly is a classic. Double-planked mahogany over cedar, with oak frames and teak decks, *Windigo* was one of the largest wooden vessels that the Hinckley yard ever built. She was commissioned by Hal Haskell of Wilmington, Delaware, who named her *Venturer* and planned to campaign her against all the top 1930s boats.

Built for speed—without sacrificing comfort—*Windigo* has had an illustrious racing career that has spanned four decades. She has won or placed well in major ocean and coastal races. Her competitors were all as famous in their day as they are today: *Bolero, Baruna, Cotton Blossom*, and *Escapade.* In her first year racing, she broke the old Bermuda Race record established by *Highland Light* in 1932 and was beaten only by *Bolero.* In 1960 she did finish first in that year's Bermuda Race. In 1962, she repeated that win, but under the name *Northern Light*, a short-lived name. In 1963 new owner Baldwin M. Baldwin changed her name to *Audacious* and moved her to California in time for the TransPac. She finished second behind *Ticonderoga*. She raced extensively on the west coast from events in Mexico to the Big Boat

Series in San Francisco. Her hull color changed from its original blue to white during this time.

She was given the name *Windigo* by Walter Gubelmann, who bought her in 1968 and headed her east again, to Oyster Bay, Long Island. He was the man who had owned for twenty years the previous *Windigo*, a 71-foot S & S yawl. During the '60s, *Windigo's* main boom was shortened when racing came under the IOR rating rules, which favored smaller mainsails more than the CCA rules.

Windigo is not only famous for her racing prowess. In 1973

Windigo *is one of the largest wooden vessels ever built by the Hinckley yard. She was built for speed and has had a racing career that has spanned four decades.*

Windigo's interior is finished in the Herreshoff tradition with varnished teak and butternut trim accenting the white-painted bulkheads.

There is a convenient pass-through between the galley and the main saloon which can be closed for formal dining.

The cabin has port and starboard upper and lower bunks, with ample built in storage.

Sandy Weld, an experienced ocean-racing sailor, acquired her to fulfill a dream of cruising to remote northern harbors. He spent nine years aboard her and wrote a book about his adventures, *Windigo, Newfoundland to Alaska.*

Todd Goodwin, a New York businessman and sailing enthusiast, bought her in 1987 from Sandy Weld. She was refastened in Maine by Wayfarer, and significant work was done on the boat by the Hinckley Yard in Maine and Pilots Point Marina in Connecticut. *Windigo* now has a shorter boom and a masthead rig. She continues to be a top contender in events such as the Antigua Classic Yacht Regatta and Antigua Race Week. In the 1996 Antigua Classic Regatta, she had a chance to test her mettle against her old adversaries *Bolero* and *Ticonderoga,* and she continues to place in modern-day races. In March 1995, Sandy Weld chartered his old love for the CCA cruise in Venezuela. Goodwin offers *Windigo* for charter in New England in the summers and the Caribbean in the winters—except when he wants to sail it himself.

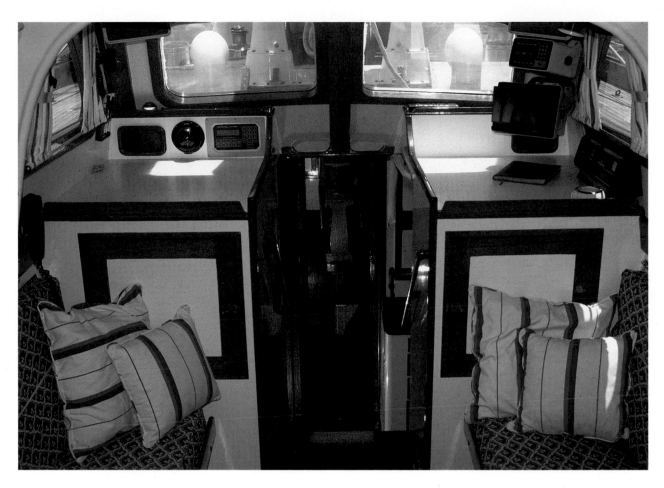

The raised deck saloon offers protection from the weather, cozy seating, and unrestricted visibility.

The cockpit is generously proportioned and extremely comfortable.

Type: Schooner
LOA: 118' (36 m)
LWL: 95' 11" (29.25 m)
Beam: 23' 9" (7.25 m)
Draft: 13' 11" (4.25 m)
Displacement: 200 tons
Hull: Alaskan cedar on teak
Designer: Garland Rotch
Builder: Nunes Brothers; Sausalito, California
Year built: 1928–30; rebuilt 1994

Z A C A

Zaca was designed by Garland Rotch, who was largely inspired by the famous Bluenose schooners, and launched in Sausalito, California, by the Nunes Brothers Boatyard the year after the stock market crash—1930—when hardly anyone was building luxury yachts. Manuel Nunes, an immigrant to the U.S. from the Azores, employed an impressive crew of workers in order to finish *Zaca* in eight months. *Zaca* was billed out at $350,000; apparently, the man who commissioned her, Templeton Crooker, a Yale-educated San Francisco banker, was undaunted by the depressed economy. He took *Zaca* around the world twice on two scientific expeditions. Crooker was keenly interested in marine biology and fitted out the boat with laboratories for experiments en route. Her voyage is chronicled by Dr. William Beebe, director of the New York Zoological Society, in a book. He describes one moment on the voyage:

> The third time the bird swept around, a shot brought it down stone dead. The *Zaca* showed her splendid maneuvering ability and turning at the moment of the shot in an astonishing small circle, she moved slowly toward the bird. Standing with a long-handled net just behind the dolphin catcher, I scooped it up and we were on our way again after a delay of only four minutes.

The first step of the round-the-world voyage was 3,000 miles to Nuku Hiva in the Marquesas. For the next two years the boat didn't stop traveling. She eventually covered 27,490 miles. After the attack on Pearl Harbor, Crooker joined the war effort and ceded *Zaca* to the U.S. Navy for $40,000, to help patrol the busy waters of San Francisco Bay. She was painted requisition gray-blue, fitted with 20mm guns and a crew of thirty-five sailors. After the war her masts were removed and surplus dealers put her up for sale, this time for $30,000. In 1945 the famed film star Errol Flynn discovered *Zaca* in a sailing magazine

This vaulted hatch has seating on both sides.

Zaca has a glorious large expansive deck with a commodious dining table amidships.

and decided he had to have her. The man of many famous characters—among them, Captain Blood, Robin Hood, the Sea Hawk, General Custer, and Don Juan—bought *Zaca* in 1946. He invested $80,000 toward her restoration, including repainting her and having new masts fitted. With all of the structural work, he was keen on refitting belowdecks; he had a projection room and a large bed installed aboard the yacht. Flynn is quoted as saying, "I want the *Zaca* to symbolize what I represent. I will hoist the image of a cock, who will crow to the four corners of the world, as my personal jack." In fact, a cock was painted on the prow.

Flynn purportedly used *Zaca* to trade gold and arms with former Nazi refuges in South America, and the story has it that Eva Peron joined him for a time, and that Fidel Castro also was a guest aboard *Zaca*. Flynn took great joy in using his yacht to entertain his friends; jaunts to Mexico, the Galapagos, and eventually to the Caribbean, having transversed the Panama Canal. The incomparable Rita Hayworth and Orson Welles appearing in the film *The Lady of Shanghai* spent five weeks aboard *Zaca* in Acapulco as a set location. *Zaca* was also involved in *Treasure in the Yucatan* and a short film, *The Cruise of Zaca*. In 1950 *Zaca* played another important role in Flynn's life when he had his honeymoon aboard with his third wife, Patrice Wymore, and apparently was caught philandering with a seventeen-year-old on his very wedding day.

In 1952 Flynn left Warner Brothers Studio, declaring, "California, go to the devil! America, go to the devil! I am going to live on the *Zaca*! Hoist the sails! Off we go!"

He based himself in Palma, Mallorca, spending time diving, going to bullfights, and entertaining international notables: Ali Khan, Farouk (former king of Egypt), Prince Rainier, and of course his old Hollywood cronies. "They came and went; I met them in casinos along the coast. We drank, we laughed—I drifted." In 1958, after much travel and partying, Flynn flew to Vancouver, Canada, in hope of selling *Zaca* to pay back his debts. He died unexpectedly of a heart attack at the age of fifty. *Zaca* remained in Mallorca, abandoned. Sean, Flynn's son with his last wife, Patrice Wymore, had no interest in *Zaca* or the sea. The boat was left to rot. In 1965 she was purchased for $40,000 by an Englishman who was enamored of her history.

The first attempt to sail her to the Côte d'Azur proved disastrous with everything falling apart—sails, fittings, engine, et cetera. The Englishman reneged on his contract and left her in disgust. She was towed to Cannes and then brought to the yard of Bernard Voisin in Villefranche-sur-Mer. Voisin purchased *Zaca* for $5,000 from Flynn's widow. *Zaca* languished in the yard for many years. In December 1988 Philippe Coussens bought the shipyard and talked about refitting *Zaca* but he never succeeded, and *Zaca* ended up sinking in the port of Beaulieu. In 1991 Roberto Memmo, an international businessman, bought the wreck of what was *Zaca* and managed to refloat her. She was towed in October 1991 from Beaulieu to the IMS Shipyard in Saint-Mandrier-sur-Mer, near Toulon. Fifty shipwrights and carpenters from Brittany were imported to restore her hull, deck, and rig. In 1992 she sailed back to the Port de Fontvieille in Monaco.

Her interior was redesigned and finished in the summer of 1994. She is quite theatrical and incredibly decorous. The aft cabin is paneled in walnut, sporting wooden pilasters with Corinthian columns, a triptych

of the Madonna, and a painted crucifix. The bathroom has a marble bathtub and vanity. The main saloon is an eclectic mix of periods with a brocade couch, marble around the fireplace, a three-footed settee in the center of the room, more wooden pilasters, and heavy brocade curtains with gilt tassels. There is incredible art including a Picasso, a few vintage guns, assorted antique chairs, and a writing desk with a lot of memorabilia from the Flynn era, including books and photos. *Zaca* made her comeback at the 1994 Monaco Classic Yacht Week. She was officially rechristened by Roberto Memmo on September 22, 1994, at a showy event that included a variety of famous personalities. The legend of *Zaca* lives on as she continues to present herself at the round of classic events in the Mediterranean.

Belowdecks, Zaca is quite an eclectic mix with antiques from a variety of periods. Brocade upholstery and curtains add an imposing feeling to the main saloon.

Her theatrical decor focuses largely on her Erroll Flynn heritage. A writing desk with books and other memorabilia commemorating his life is permanently displayed. The owner's stateroom is paneled in walnut, sporting wooden pilasters with Corinthian columns, a triptych of the Madonna and a painted crucifix. The guest cabins are a little more sedate in their decor.

Type: Schooner
LOA: 143' 8" (43.80 m)
LOD: 124' 8" (38 m)
Beam: 23' 6" (7.2 m)
Draft: 14' (4.28 m)
Displacement: 175 tons
Hull: Steel
Designer: Olivier F. van Meer;
* Enkhuizen, Holland*
Builder: Amstel Shipyard; Amstel, Holland
Year built: 1992
Engine: Rolls Royce 8 cyl. 300 hp

ZACA A TE MOANA

Zaca a te Moana is a new classic, commissioned by Dutch businessman and entrepreneur Ed Kastelein in 1991. Although this yacht is often compared to Errol Flynn's *Zaca*, she is completely different. The only similarity is the first part of her name—and perhaps a modicum of inspiration. Her name literally means "peace of the sea" in Samoan. Kastelein chose Dutch naval architect Olivier F. van Meer as the designer and worked closely with him and his firm to achieve his dream boat. The word "classic" was key from the inception of the boat. The hull is beautifully proportioned, and the gaff rig is as decorous today as it was during the golden age of yachting. The boat was built at the Shipyard De Amstel BV, in Ouderkerk a/d Amstel. The hull is welded steel with a teak deck on a steel frame. The bulwark, heavy gunwale, hatches, and doors are teak and were made and fitted by Scheepstimmerbedrijf HvC of Enkhuizen.

Kastelein has had a love for classics his whole life. He previously owned two very famous boats, *Aile Blanche* and *Thendara*. Kastelein is a hands-on skipper/owner. In developing his schooner, he told his naval architect, "I want to avoid gadgets—to sail with sailors, not engineers. Also, I want to use instruments rather than computers." A boat such as *Zaca a te Moana* had not been built in Holland in over forty years. As classic as she is on deck, she does have a few modern conveniences, such as hydraulics. On charter she can be sailed with a crew of six, which includes Ed and his wife Sophie.

Belowdecks *Zaca a te Moana* has a completely open, contemporary feel to her. Her main saloon is a very generous space, using the full beam of the boat, and has a lot of light. Her interior has a satin-finished maple paneling offset by red-leather settees and custom brass fittings. Forward of the saloon is a modern utilitarian service galley with a laundry and

Zaca a te Moana's graceful hull and elegant sail plan are truly reminiscent of the beautiful gaff-rigged schooners from the turn-of-the-century that inspired her design.

storage area opposite. Aft near the companionway is a small office and navigation station. There are three roomy two berth cabins with en suite bathrooms and one grand owner's stateroom with a large canopied bed.

With 800 square meters of sail area, *Zaca a te Moana* is quick to accelerate—she can easily reach 10 knots when under sail. Since her launching she has joined the classic fleet at the Nioulargue Race. From afar, it is impossible to discern *Zaca a te Moana* from the true "old" classics. In the fall of 1996, Kastelein sold his dream boat—perhaps to build another…

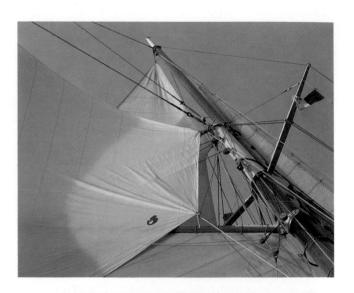

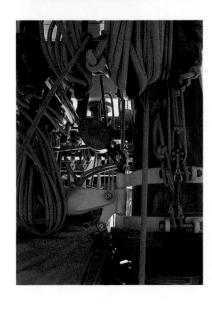

The magnificent master stateroom
extends the full beam and has a queen-
size bed, built-in cupboards with plenty
of storage. Due to the extremely high
headroom, there is a grand sense of
space in this cabin.

The vanity in the master stateroom has
cabinets inlaid with burled maple.

Belowdeck belies the traditional exterior in that it is light and contemporary in design and feel. The huge open main saloon is paneled in satin-finished maple. The dining chairs and settees are upholstered in red leather which provides a stunning contrast to the light wood.

Type: Yawl
LOA: 82' (25 m)
LWL: 57' 7" (17.57 m)
Beam: 17' 6" (5.35 m)
Draft: 8' 6" (2.6 m)
Displacement: 39.6 tons
Hull: Cedar and mahogany
Designers: Steve Dalzell and Edwin Meayers
Builder: Southampton Yacht Services;
  Southampton, England
Year built: 1995
Engine: Caterpillar 3-106 215 hp.

ZANNA

Zanna has been described as a high-tech blue-water cruiser with an Edwardian heart. Since *Zanna* is the owner's seventh boat, he knew what he wanted: an elegant "classic"—with long overhangs and clear decks—that was fast, sea-kindly, and capable of being handled by a small crew. The accommodation would consist of a full-beam saloon, navigation area, three twin or double en suite guest cabins, a sizeable fully-equipped galley, and a twin-berth crew-cabin forward. A yawl rig was specified for its flexibility both at sea and at anchor—a fully battened mainsail and mizzen for efficiency. A large lazarette was required to stow a fully-inflated dinghy underdeck as well as equipment and spares for long-distance cruising. The machinery space was to be of adequate size to enable all the systems to be reached and serviced. The owner even dictated the overall length, beam, and draft specifications—the latter to be an absolute maximum of nine feet. The naval architect, Steve Dalzell (chief lecturer in marine naval architecture at the University of Southampton), worked many computer hours to fit all the components together. A model underwent a full series of tank tests.

Zanna was built at Southampton Yacht Services, chosen because of the experience of its skilled woodworkers and its reputation for restoring vintage yachts. The backbone and frames of the boat are laminated Brazilian mahogany. The core planking is western red cedar with four outer veneers of cedar and a

fifth of khaya mahogany. The outer epoxy coating includes a non-structural layer of fiberglass to improve abrasion resistance. The deck itself is ply overlaid with epoxy-bonded teak without mechanical fastenings, and each plank snaped into king planks or covering boards in the old tradition. On deck, brightly varnished coamings, hatches, doghouse, companionways, dorade boxes, and skylights are all in solid teak—radiused, dovetailed and constructed in the shop before being fitted onboard.

Zanna *competed in the 1996 Antigua Classic Yacht Regatta in the Spirit of Tradition Class. She proved herself to be extremly fast and was only beaten by the much larger* Alejandra *and* Adela.

Belowdecks owes much of its design to the eighteenth century. The paneling in the main saloon is Brazilian mahogany with Madrona panels, inlaid with ebony.

The main saloon table is an ingenious piece of furniture that extends for dining, converts to a games board and incorporates a secret liquor cabinet.

Zanna is not old, having been launched in the fall of 1995, yet she is most definitely a classic. Her long bow and stern overhangs are reminiscent of classic ocean-racing yachts, but her modern fin and bulb keel throw weight low down to allow for a tall rig. The spars made by GMT in the States, are carbon-fiber, painted to simulate a wood-grain effect.

The interior owes much of its design to the eighteenth century. The wood is Brazilian mahogany with Madrona panels (from the burr wood of the American strawberry tree) inlaid with ebony. Moldings and other elements have been kept small and delicate; door handles and hinges are faithfully copied from eighteenth-century originals. The fiddles and the companionway stairs are reminiscent of Fife. The main saloon table is an exquisite and ingenious piece of furniture that extends for dining, converts to a game board, and incorporates a secret liquor cabinet. The saloon cabinets are finished with "Regency" brass latticing and pleated silk. A brass-barred skylight filters light into the main saloon, and brass globe lights illuminate the polished paneling. The design for screw-type skylight lifters were literally borrowed from *Ticonderoga*. Since S.Y.S. had restored the famous Herreshoff, they were able to take a pattern from the original! The owner's stateroom is paneled in bird's-eye maple. The cabin door was a woodworking challenge since one side is maple and the other side is teak.

All of *Zanna* has been thoughtfully conceived and beautifully executed. Her first season out, she raced successfully—and won—in the "Spirit of Tradition" class at the 1996 Antigua Classic Yacht Regatta. In her first 10,000 miles, *Zanna*, a modern classic, has lived up to the expectations of her owner, designer, and builder.

Because of the fine detailing, the navigation station could more aptly be called the executive office.

The master suite is paneled in bird's-eye maple. It has twin beds, ample storage space, and an en suite bathroom.

Type: Motor yacht
LOA: 60' (18.29 m)
LWL: 54' 9" (16.68 m)
Beam: 12' (3.65 m)
Draft: 3' 6" (1.06 m)
Hull: Mahogany and yellow pine:
Builder: New York Yacht, Launch & Engine Co.;
* Morris Heights, New York*
Year built: 1913, rebuilt 1996
Engine: Caterpillar 3116, 350 hp

ZAPALA

apala was built in 1913 as *Sispud II* by the New York Yacht, Launch & Engine Company of Morris Heights, New York, for Mr. Joseph B. Cousins Esq. of the Manhasset Bay Yacht Club. She is 60 feet overall in length, built of long-leaf yellow pine planking on steam bent white oak frames. She was originally powered with a 4-cylinder, 50 hp twentieth-century gasoline marine engine. She has the distinction of being one of the last remaining examples of the early gasoline-powered yachts built prior to World War I.

Sispud II had a long history of colorful owners. One of them was James Adams, owner of the James Adams Floating Theater. Mr. Adams's theater was towed around to coastal towns of the South, bringing entertainment and culture to isolated areas, until it finally sank in Thunderbolt, Georgia, in 1941. *Sispud II* followed the theater to all of its destinations. Edna Ferber created her novel *Show Boat*, later to become a smash Broadway play, from her experiences living aboard and traveling with Adams on *Sispud II*.

Sispud II was well maintained until the late 1970s. In the 1980s she was abandoned out of the water in a backwoods boatyard. In 1990 Earl McMillen took an interest in her, and after acquiring her, moved her to a building in Fairhaven, Massachusetts. His company, McMillen Yachts, along with a group of enthusiastic partners, completed a thorough eight-month renovation on her in 1995-96. She was completely reframed, and all her planks below the waterline were restacked. Everything from her deck on up

is new. Her pilothouse has been redesigned and the hatches, handrails, and canopy have all been refabricated. The original interior remains intact; however, the mahogany paneling was refinished. All the hardware is original. She has a completely new mechanical system—a modern Caterpillar 3116, 350 hp engine was installed along with an exceptionally long shaft to accommodate the engine which is far forward. McMillen changed her name to *Zapala*, which is the Spanish name of Georgia's Sapelo Island.

Bow-to-stern restoration of Zapala *took eight months. Her hull, which was long leaf yellow pine below the water line and cedar above the waterline, was completely dried out from years of sitting out of the water. She was reframed with white oak and all her planks were restacked below the waterline. Everything above deck—hatches, handrails, pilot house—are brand new.*

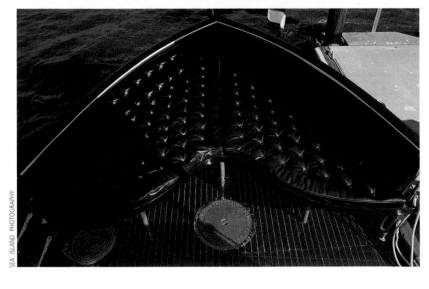

The canoe stern sports a newly fabricated V-shaped settee.

The interior was removed, refurbished and put back into the boat. All of the wood is mahogany below. The main saloon has two decorative columns with Corinthian capitals on the forward bulkhead.

A classic vessel, whether old or new, is much more than a particular aesthetic or construction technique. It is a synthesis of proven design principles, traditional technologies, experienced seamanship, and historical continuity. Lines for most classic vessels were laid down in an era when cultural aesthetic standards were infinitely more rigorous than they are today. Furthermore, designers and builders of the time deeply respected the lessons of the past and were slow to adopt untested forms and methods. These concerns resulted in workaday fishing and cargo boats of stunning beauty, ingenious practicality, and remarkable performance. Yachts were vastly outnumbered by workboats and were strongly influenced by the evolution of their working sisters.

As form evolved, so did construction methods, hand in glove. The highly individualized, craft-oriented production of wooden vessels resisted the centralization of big business and has remained, in the end, largely a local industry. It requires more skill than machinery, more experience than training, and remains a noble historical tradition, a vital link to our past. To reject traditional wooden-vessel construction while maintaining a classic aesthetic does no more than create a classic 'look.' While this is no doubt preferable to a modern 'look,' it is surely not classic. Why not choose a construction method that is simple, practical, durable, beautiful, and historical? Why not choose to build a classic?

Fortunately, there remains a small cadre of folks who were not swayed by the consumerism that created the modern plastic yacht. This small group created a quiet movement that became a revival by the mid-1980s. It was no pendulum swing, but for someone who wished to avoid the spiritual bankruptcy of the production fiberglass yacht, there was now an alternative. These folks continued to build, rebuild, and maintain vessels crafted in the traditional manner. They continued to look for boats with real aesthetic appeal, proven design characteristics, and the feel of a proper vessel. They were not deterred by lack of insurance, and they managed without ready bank financing. But most importantly, they were not afraid of maintenance.

The practicality of the maintenance of a traditional wooden boat is rarely discussed, even by its proponents. The technology is simple and accessible. Almost anyone can learn how to repair any part of their boat—and repair it exactly as good as new. It requires few tools and widely available materials. If a sound, well-built boat is washed down with salt water regularly, allowed to ventilate properly, and kept adequately painted, it will last a long time. And when decay of one sort or another sets in, in one place or another, she can be dragged up the beach and—piece by piece, year by year—replaced until she is entirely new. In the process, her owner would have remade a part of him or herself, as well.

Although the fleet of classic wooden yachts is undoubtedly larger and more vital than it was some thirty years ago, it now appears to be under siege once again, at least in America. What is most discouraging is that this latest attack is coming from within the wooden boat revival itself. The wooden boat community is polarizing around the 'old' and the 'new' technologies, and, once again, the 'new' is winning. Modern epoxy-based, wood-composite construction is increasingly marketed as superior in strength, practicality, and durability to traditional plank-on-frame methods, even for repair of traditional construction. This misconception is extremely damaging to professional builders of plank-on-frame vessels and to the classic vessels themselves, and it forces a debate on what it is that makes a vessel a classic and what it is that makes a classic worth preserving.

Gary S. Maynard, Martha's Vineyard, Massachusetts
G.S. Maynard & Company
Builder, restorer, purist, owner and restorer of Violet

Ross Gannon and I started Gannon & Benjamin Marine Railways for a host of reasons. An excuse to continue 'just messing about in boats' is as valid as any, although I must qualify 'boats' to be unconditionally built of wood in the traditional manner. We both owned old wooden boats and needed a place to work on them. In 1979 an attempted McDonald's hamburger franchise for this location was driven out of town (and off the island) by public outcry. We approached the new owner of the vacated waterfront property and soon signed a lease to build and operate a boatyard. We dove right in, despite the advice of many doubtful businessmen, and have been swimming along ever since—heads above water, mostly. Our first canvas-back gaff sloop was launched in 1980.

After nearly thirty years of continuous involvement with wooden sailing craft, I am more convinced than ever that a plank-on-frame vessel is the ultimate in yacht construction. Not only does this method produce an enduring vessel with integrity, heart and soul, but it also requires a process that is so ancient and noble as to inspire the builder to work above his ability, to continue challenging himself in his expression of the rarest combination of science and art.

According to Webster, the word 'classic' properly defines a vessel designed and serving as a 'standard of excellence' with an additional caveat of equal import to be 'enduring and traditional.' In an age when 'classic' is so grossly distorted as to encompass an amorphous range of social unconsciousness from Coca Cola to a popular sitcom, we must remind ourselves of the real meaning of the word. 'Classic' should not define external glitter any more than 'world class' should describe a hamburger. A 'classic yacht' must represent a graceful and well-proportioned hull whose individual parts are not only enduring but are created by a traditional process of skill and inspiration. A classic yacht speaks to you in a distinct and compelling voice.

Nathaniel Benjamin, Martha's Vineyard, Massachusetts
Specialist in wooden boats
Gannon & Benjamin Marine Railway

The Gannon & Benjamin Yard • Candle in the Wind *and* Sally May, *new classics built by G&B.*
Ross in Tern, *a new Rosinante* • *Hard at work* • *Ross's son Lyle on a harbor jaunt with Bushhog on bow watch.*

Solway Maid was launched in October of 1940, in a world which had gone mad, in which every ship launched was painted the dullest shade of gray. The quiet unceremonious launching of a sleek, white-hulled, 20-ton yacht at the celebrated slipways of William Fife & Sons passed with little fuss. And yet it must have been a poignant moment for her creator, William Fife. He was in his 84th year, the third and final generation of this Scottish yacht-building dynasty founded in the early nineteenth century on the shallow sloping beach at Fairlie on the Firth of Clyde. His yard had been requisitioned by the British Admiralty as a research establishment, and by the time war clouds had cleared, Fife had already taken his final departure, passing away at the grand old age of 88 in 1944.

And so the final launching by William Fife & Sons, yard #825—"A Thirty Five Foot Waterline Fast Cruising Cutter Suitable for Ocean Racing"—laid down speculatively in 1939 as a stock boat, became "Solway Maid," named after the cruising grounds on the south coast of Scotland, much loved by her purchaser F. Ivan Carr. After visiting Fairlie, Carr wrote, "She made my mouth water. I inquired the price, which seemed like the National Debt, and went home. But could I forget her? Came the War, and the price was less—quite a lot less. We bought her as she lay."

There would always have been a wonderfully visual counterpoint in Fife's building sheds as his designs came alive at the hands of his skilled workforce; things of great beauty going through their birth pangs in the most austere surroundings. That piquancy must have been all the more sublime when Carr first set eyes on this mouth-watering example of functional art, her superbly fair hull—smelling sweetly of newly applied enamel and varnish—standing alone on the empty building shed which had given birth to countless yachts. This one was the last of the line.

Solway Maid, like Fife's fast cruisers, was, in effect, a cruising version of the International Rule meter boats, but she was unhindered by a rating rule. It is quite common for admirers to ask which 8-meter she is when they come alongside. But to the practiced and knowledgeable eye, it is easy to see in her the simple pertness which Fife modeled into his later cruising designs. She has more beam; a more delicious sweep to her sheer, giving higher—but never too high—freeboard; slightly more moderate overhangs; and a more sturdy masthead rig, simple, "eyesweet." Her coachroof is never too high, beautifully finished in mahogany and faithfully following the sweep of her mahogany covering board; the hollow spruce mast is raked at an angle that suggests she's straining at her mooring—eager to go places fast. And for thirty-odd years, with her, Ivan Carr, *Solway Maid* did go many places—and she was fast.

Carr died in 1974. *Solway Maid* had become a ship of memories, perhaps a mausoleum—a monument to summer days past, friendships made, even marriages created. For Marjorie Carr, Ivan Carr's second wife, the memories were just too strong to part with her. So she lay in storage, not forgotten—admired and coveted by all who walked past her elegant form—but denied her natural element. In 1987, the Carr family finally sold *Solway Maid* to Englishman Rodger Sandiford. The boat has been thoughtfully and lovingly restored and Sandiford has the same respect for her that Carr had. Built speculatively as a stock boat, *Solway Maid* performs incredibly well in bad weather and difficult seas. She was not built as a racer, yet she is quite competitive at the classic yacht regattas. She was not built as a luxury cruiser, yet she has logged many cruising miles. Ivan Carr used to write cruising articles for *Yachting Monthly* magazine and he introduced his pieces with an old North of England saying, "Choose an old dog for a long road." *Solway Maid* has certainly proved it. She holds the memory of cruises past and looks set to outlive all those who are lucky enough to sail on her today. She should stand as a fitting tribute to her designer for many a year to come and remain a constant companion for that long road.

Iain McAllister, U.K. and Denmark
Skipper of Solway Maid

The definition of a classic—that is a difficult one! My dictionary says:

• work of recognized excellence

• appeals to educated taste

• worthy of imitation

My thoughts are that not all old yachts are classic. To be a 'classic' a yacht has to have a certain elegance, be appealing to the eye and just look right. I feel that there is a great difference between wooden boats and classic yachts. This difference existed when they were built and in my mind still exists now. A wooden boat is to me a working vessel, warship, fishing boat, et cetera, and a yacht, wooden or otherwise, is a pleasure craft.

As to why and how I became involved in classic-yacht restoration: I sailed for pleasure from the age of one. When career decisions had to be made, there didn't seem to be a life in sailing. I went to the university and obtained a degree in production engineering. After university I became involved with the family business, rapidly becoming disillusioned and leaving after two years. I met John Bardon and became one of the original crew on *Jessica*. I lasted on *Jessica* eighteen months, leaving as mate. I then joined Paul Goss on *Belle Aventure*. When the *Altair* job came up, I went with Paul and became involved in my first major restoration.

I left *Altair* at the end of the restoration and worked with Tracey Edwards and rebuilt *Maiden* for her. Shortly after that, Mr. Obrist and I got together and started Fairlie Restorations. When *Altair* was at S.Y.S., it became apparent that an established yard, whilst being excellent for a new build, was not altogether the best way to approach a restoration. The philosophy of restoration work is not the same as normal yacht work.

Duncan Walker, Hamble, U.K.
Manager, Fairlie Yacht Restorations

Duncan Walker at the helm of Fulmar *at Monaco Classic Week.*

In August of 1989, *Endeavour* and *Shamrock V*, two Charles Nicholson America's Cup challengers from the '30s, raced in the waters off Newport, Rhode Island. It was the first time two J's had raced since 1937. To the sailors onboard the boats and to the spectators afloat and ashore, it was a moment they had never expected to see.

Now there are three J-Class sloops—*Shamrock V, Velsheda,* and *Endeavour*—and three 23 meters—*Cambria, Candida,* and *Astra*—restored and in good sailing condition. But they are only six prominent examples of a growing fleet of restored classics in the world today.

In addition to these behemoths, there are hundreds of wonderful, smaller power, sail, paddle, and rowing yachts being restored all over the world. It seems there is a growing group of people who recognize the great value and beauty in these vessels. At last!

All of us restoration fanatics are familiar with the feelings of miserable panic about the loss of our yachting heritage. Despite our efforts, we've all watched helplessly as boats were cut up and scrapped, sunk or burned for insurance, or have rotted into compost. But now it seems to me that these nightmare occurrences have slowed down. Classic yachts are *finally* being recognized as the rare, historical artifacts they are.

With the growing classic fleet has come the need for shipwrights trained in the specialized techniques of restoring and maintaining yachts. Many yards—Fairlie Restoration, Narragansett Shipwrights, and Southampton Yacht Services, to name a few—are constantly on the lookout for restoration craftsmen.

To fill this need, to rescue and restore as many boats as possible, and to create public awareness of our yachting heritage, a number of yachtsmen, businessmen, and educators formed the International Yacht Restoration School (IYRS) in Newport, Rhode Island. We believe it is the only yacht restoration school in the country and one of the few in the world. In 1995 IYRS obtained a 2½ -acre waterfront site in downtown Newport, including a huge old electric generating plant that is now the IYRS Restoration Hall. In June 1996 IYRS began teaching classes structured around the complete restoration of a variety of vessels. Currently, IYRS is just completing the restoration of a Nathaniel Herreshoff S-boat, a Chris Craft gasoline-driven runabout, two gaff-rigged Beetle cats, and a double-ended Peapod rowboat. In an effort to spread the good word about our yachting heritage, all restoration work at IYRS is open to the public, free of charge.

IYRS's future flagship and most important restoration project is the 1885 130-foot schooner *Coronet*. Built by the Poillon Yard in Brooklyn, New York, for New York Yacht Club member Rufus Bush, *Coronet* spent the first twenty years of her life racing and cruising around the world. Among her many exploits are a voyage to Japan in 1895 to serve as transport for the first joint Japanese-American scientific expedition, and a brilliant win in the 1887 transatlantic race against *Dauntless*. From 1905 to 1995, *Coronet* made missionary voyages around the world.

IYRS is off to a good start. It remains to be seen whether it will fulfill its promise and become an enduring bastion of yachting preservation. Y'all come visit, hear?

Elizabeth Meyer, Newport, Rhode Island
Owner of Endeavour,
Yacht restoration and management consultant
Founder of International Yacht Restoration School

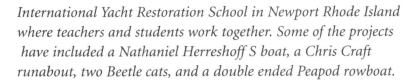

International Yacht Restoration School in Newport Rhode Island where teachers and students work together. Some of the projects have included a Nathaniel Herreshoff S boat, a Chris Craft runabout, two Beetle cats, and a double ended Peapod rowboat.

247

S.Y.S. was formed in the old C & N shipyard in Northam, Southampton, in 1980 when the C & N yard closed. Piers Wilson started the company with the best of the remaining skilled men still left at the yard. Piers was the C & N production director and felt that the wealth of the local yacht-building and repairing skills should not be lost. He started the new company with an order to complete a new 90-foot sloop that had already been started by C & N.

Piers's policy was to sell skilled hours together with effective management and not to sell boats. He thought it was better to promote the local skills available, with a policy of training young men in the traditional skills of joinery and shipwrighting by encouraging a continuous program of apprenticeships with the local training colleges.

The policy worked, and since 1980 a number of yacht captains and owners heard about S.Y.S., and yachts came to Southampton from all over the world for repairs and refits. Among them was *Altair*, which had suffered many hardships and certain modernization during a long life in the Mediterranean. Her new owner was keen to restore her as accurately as possible, and Piers together with the captain spent a great deal of energy researching the details of joinery styles and other typical features. Extensive structural repairs were needed to bring this fine schooner back into first-class condition. Certain modern equipment such as engines, generators, and refrigeration, were carefully installed without compromising the look of the ship. *Altair*'s owner was exceptional in that he accepted the expense of recasting the keel to compensate for the extra weight of new equipment without changing the trim of the yacht.

Further restorations and refits followed, some of which required a terrific attention to detail since the original interiors had been lost or altered. *Thendara* was a particular example, where this fine 1930s Mylne-designed yacht had been through two owners who had started a restoration program before a third owner finally completed the project. S.Y.S. received an empty hull in reasonable condition with a partially complete but substandard deck. The project was designed around the owner's budget and based on the style of the original layout to cope with modern requirements for on-site bathrooms and more privacy for female crew members than was typical in the 1930s.

Modern epoxy glues and long-lasting marine-quality plywood are used to ensure a sound subdeck, and other structural components are laminated since grown knees, and the like, are difficult and expensive to find. These modern kinds of materials benefit the integrity of the vessel and are usually undetectable to the casual viewer. Other little details, such as rebated silicon rubber seals in the skylights and hatches, help to keep them watertight.

Restorations and refits to pedigree classic yachts are always the subject of criticism by purists. The term *restoration* should only really be applied to a project that is being reasonably accurately restored and due condition is being applied to the originality of the vessel. Refits are projects where repairs and alterations have little regard for historical accuracy but are required to keep the vessel seaworthy and in a functioning condition acceptable to the owner. The owner is the key to everything, and we at S.Y.S. exist because of their yachting needs and aspirations.

The 'classic' debate can be long and drawn out. My personal view is that a 'classic' yacht is almost any yacht from the past that has the abilities and looks to make someone want to preserve it. I should qualify this with the thought that such a vessel should have traditional looks and a touch of the past about her. New classic yachts are those that replicate some of those looks from the past. Most of the Bruce King yachts come into this category. Classic yachts of the future will possibly include the old Swan 65s, Nicholson 70s, and Hinckleys, but I doubt that the new extreme high-tech Wally types will ever be considered 'classic.'

Peter Davies, Southampton, U.K.
Director, Southampton Yacht Services

As a person who owns and has restored five vintage sail and power yachts over 60 feet, I guess you could say I'm an incurable romantic and passionate about these vessels. I look upon period yachts as artistic pieces, a form of functional sculpture. Just as a painting has its artistic style, so each classic yacht has its pedigree.

The period I find most attractive is the turn-of-the-century up through the 1930s or until World War II. That short span of time produced some of the finest, most beautiful yachts, the likes of which we will never see again. Of the thousands built during this era, most are now gone. Time is running out. Most of the precious few yachts remaining will not survive beyond this generation without some care or proper restoration. I find it extremely gratifying to rescue a beautiful vessel and save it from extinction.

One contributing factor to the disappearance of classic boats is the increasing value of waterfront real estate. Boatyards are no longer willing to allow an old derelict to take up space in the back lot year after year. Sadly, in my lifetime I've seen hundreds of great old vessels chain sawed and bulldozed.

Some of the things that make up a good pedigree are: the designer (responsible for the beauty of the lines and the success of the design), the builder (who selects the quality of the materials and controls the details of his artisans), and the history. Who owned her? What stories survive? Which races did she win? The fun in restoring and owning a vintage yacht is digging up leads on former families, locating old photographs, and discovering old stories.

My philosophy in restoration is to retain as much of the original fabric as possible and to strive toward the original design in every aspect of the yacht. First priority is to reproduce the original whenever anything needs repair or replacement. This includes masts, interior layout, and hardware (from light fixtures and doorknobs to winches on deck). I believe it is these little details that give an antique yacht her personality. "The sum of the parts is greater than the whole." Unfortunately, sometimes there must be compromises in order to comply with U.S. Coast Guard certification. However, I enjoy going to great pains to make patterns and cast many fittings. It certainly would be much easier to buy modern items off the shelf, which seems to be the trend for our instant gratification society.

Today we see great care taken with regard toward originality in accurate restoration of classic automobiles, runabouts, grand houses, and even airplanes. We have yet to see any decent number of larger yachts restored in this way. All too often in this day and age, we see boats restored to a particular owner's whims. In many cases a yacht that has survived many generations intact has her original interior gutted and thrown away, original spars and sail plans replaced in the interest of speed, followed by keel replacement to suit the new sail plan. Usually modern winches are installed along with a new interior layout to suit the present owner. What remains of the original artifact? Maybe the hull, which at this point may as well be replaced, perhaps made more efficient with carbon fiber and a new design! What usually happens next is the owner sells the boat within a few years. The original boat is now lost forever.

The field of classic-yacht restoration lacks educational leadership. Most of the influence placed on yacht restorers today is from the vendors looking to sell some new product to the enthusiasts. Magazines on the subject are supported by the modern vendor's advertising dollar. However, there is hope with the recent birth of the International Yacht Restoration School in Newport, R.I. and the leadership of the Antique and Classic Boat Society (A.C.B.S.) in Clayton, New York. Other good news is that several fine, pure restorations are taking place in Europe, including many American vessels. This is inspiration and an example for us all.

Bob Tiedemann, Newport, Rhode Island
Owner and restorer of classic yachts:
Gleam, Mariner, Northern Light, M/V Pam, *and* l'Allegro

Although I am the owner and general manager of F.A.P.A. S.p.A., a major company involved in the production of car parts, I am passionate about classic boats. This passion came to fruition in 1986, when I acquired *Nordwind*, a 1939, 86-foot yacht. Then in 1990 I decided to devote myself to the restoration of classic boats and, for this reason, I established a shipyard in Porto Ferraio, where a full-time crew of ten spends all of its time restoring the different boats I have purchased during the last ten years.

Though I love classic boats in general, I hold motorboats in the greatest esteem. To my way of thinking, this kind of boat has a peculiarity that must be taken into particular consideration: While sailing boats are practically designed by the wind and the sea, which standardize their shapes, motorboats, whose propulsion is from an engine, allow the designer notable exercise of style and fantasy.

For me, collecting and restoring classic motorboats has been and still is a wonderful experience, which has contributed to the bringing back to the history of yachting some important boats. The next step will be the establishment of a permanent museum for classic boats somewhere on the Mediterranean coast.

Ugo Baravalle
Restorer of classic boats, Italy

Islay—*winner of the 1996 Monaco Classic Week concours d'élegance.*

Islay *in the process of her renovation.*

Ugo Baravalle.

Islay *sparkling after all the work was done.*

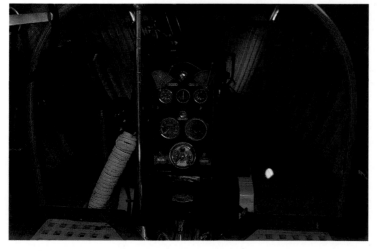

The popularity of classic yachts, and old wooden boats in general, started in Italy in the mid-'70s, reaching its peak in the mid-'80s. In fact, during this period, not only were classic power and sailboats popular, but also automobiles, motor bikes and airplanes. For some reason, there was a new surge of interest in restoring boats over 40 years old. This 'fashion' for classic yachts, started by some wealthy Italians, had become after a few years, a cultural phenomenon giving birth to a new generation of naval architects, riggers, and shipyards who began to specialize in restoration.

Italy was in an excellent position to be at the forefront of yacht restoration, as many classic yachts flew the Italian flag. A number of shipyards with skilled workers who had worked on traditional yachts were available to work on these large masterpieces. Among these were Beconcini, Valdettaro, Argentario, Monfalcone, and Sangermani. In the early '80s, ahead of most European countries, Italy was re-launching fully restored yachts such as *Croce del Sud, Orion, Mariette, Astra, Candida, Silvia, Joyette, Black Swan,* and *Vagrant*. Also, the first large classic yacht event to take place in the Mediterranean was the 1982 Veteran Boat Rally in Porto Cervo, Sardinia

Along with the larger classics, a number of smaller, historically important boats were also undergoing a rebirth: *Alzavola, Blue Peter, Vistona, Tirrenia, Emilia, Cintra, Kipawa, Tonino,* and *Moya*. In the mid '80s, all the Italian shipyards were so busy that the Italian owner of *Creole* had to take her 'abroad.'

At present, several yards are working on restoring classics—newly launched at Beconcini is the 130-foot *Te Vega*. Thanks to the ongoing activity and interest in classic yachts, a new generation of carpenters and craftsmen have found their calling, keeping sacred the traditional Italian skill in restoring and the taste in refurbishing.

Erik Pascoli, Monaco
Judge, Monaco Classic Yacht Week
Project manager for the refit of Mariette *and* Astra *in the 1980s*

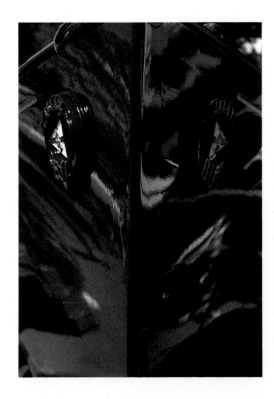

PHOTOGRAPHS COMPLIMENTS OF UGO BARAVALLE

The appeal or enjoyment, as well as value, of pleasure boats comes primarily from two sources: first, the pleasures gained from the act of sailing and its independent way of life; second, the visual aesthetic pleasures of a yacht's appearance. There are many different stylistic approaches, but design aesthetics generally take place at three levels.

The first, or fundamental, level is the establishment of the basic proportions, combined with sizing and arranging the visual masses of the primary design elements. The visual masses are usually driven by utility requirements, or possibly a rating rule, as well as basic principles of design. If a design fails at this fundamental level—if it has bad proportions or if the visual masses lack balance—the highest level of aesthetic evolution will never be attained. Further development will be limited to damage control, visual diversionary tactics, or generally attempting to make the most of an unfortunate situation. Sadly, designers are frequently required to operate at this level.

Once the visual masses have been established, the second level of aesthetic design is to wrap them in curves and surfaces. Perhaps one of the reasons boats can be such visually appealing objects is that their shapes are derived primarily from curved lines, giving them perhaps a greater connection with natural forms than most other man-made objects. When arranging the curves and surfaces of a design, I believe that lines must flow with direction and purpose. Spirals, cyma curves, and conic sections impart motion and excitement, while circles, arcs, and straight lines do not. Parallel and flat sections generally lack interest. Twisting, winding, and reverse curves create drama. Finding the right balance between visual drama and restraint is perhaps one of the most difficult issues facing the designer. There should be a balance between curved and straight, rounded and defined, masculine and feminine.

The third level of aesthetic design relates to intangibles. It is at this level that designer individuality is most apparent and a designer has the most power to elicit a strong emotional response from the viewer. The visual elements that make up a yacht design interact in concert—as with a musical composition, the total is always greater than the sum of its parts. It is this intangible essence of totality that determines the third level aesthetic value of a design. Make one seemingly small change on a truly harmonious design, and frequently any artistic summits will vanish. The dimensional differences between good design and bad can be very small, indeed. Many times they are no more than fractions of an inch. Often design errors are so subtle that many people are not consciously aware of them, but on an intuitive level one knows that something is amiss.

When working with buyers who desire a technically modern functioning yacht, but one whose styling reflects an earlier age, additional aesthetic issues must be addressed. Traditional yachts were usually built of wood. Certainly the joinery was wood—a vanishing art developed over time to minimize the dimensional instability of wood in conditions of varying temperature and humidity. Translating a traditional design to a modern yacht requires awareness of traditional joinery methods and an understanding of the technical reasons behind these methods.

We have always believed, where yachts are concerned, that technology and utility are only part of the story. To fulfill both the utility and technology requirements, and to do so in a manner encompassing as much visual satisfaction as possible, must be the goal of a skilled designer. Technology is fleeting; it is constantly changing. Aesthetic beauty is timeless, and it alone provides the motivation for preservation. It is hoped that as present technology gives way to the new, we have been able to impart to our designs enough appeal, both tangible and intangible, that will allow them to endure.

Bruce King, Newcastle, Maine
Naval Architect, Yacht Designer

At the age of eleven, I found I was incapable of conjugating any Latin verb other than *amo*, and took up the practical skills of woodworking instead. Three years later I met an antique dealer in Winchester who appeared to me to have the most perfect job, selling antiques and restoring furniture. This meeting set the path for a life with antique furniture. At the age of sixteen, I met John White, then Managing Director of Camper & Nicholsons who changed my views again by introducing me to some spectacular yachts. I was particularly awed by the 212-foot *Shemara*. Later that year, when I went to train at the London College of Furniture, I knew I wanted to be involved not only in furniture, but also in yachting. By 1970 I found myself working with John White at Camper & Nicholsons, and *Shemara* was still in the yard. My office today is only twenty paces away from where I was in 1970.

When asked to come up with some thoughts on the definition of what a classic yacht is, I can offer the following: classic yacht design stems from traditional methods, the use of natural materials employed for their strength in construction and beauty, shaped by the craftsmen to be an integral part of the yacht's function. Together, these give the yacht spirit and practicality related to its time. With timber-constructed yachts, the frames, knees, beams and carlings are all visible, and their strength and purpose are obvious.

A Fife yacht built at Fairlie's will have tongue, bead and groove bulkheads, as that was the logical material to use to shape and attach to the frames. With steel construction, much of the frame is covered, nevertheless you can still see the decks attached to the angle beams. As the yachts became larger, the structure became less visible and paneling covered the linings and bulkheads.

Still, with any yacht refit, replicated, or newly built in traditional materials, we would expect to see some part of the structure, as that is key to how everything in the interior must relate to each other. Refitting *Ticonderoga* at Southampton Yacht Services in 1988–89 gave me the great advantage of being able to look over Herreshoff's shoulder—he always intended for "*Ti*" to have a cruising interior and was dismayed when she was stripped out for racing.

Yachting of the '20s provided some incredible interiors which reflected the owner's tastes and lifestyle—the way they entertained and relaxed in what became their country home at sea. They would bring their furniture, carpets, and pianos onboard only to remove them at the end of each season when the yacht was laid up. Without the obsessions of these incredible people we would not have these legends today, nor would we have the sponsorship to maintain our craft.

Endeavour is an extraordinary story of reconstruction, maintaining the overall perception, beauty and majestic performance of the original vessel. This image, carefully retained but using new materials, engines, generators, winches, and operating with a reduced crew, completes the conversion from the great America's Cup challenger to one of the most beautiful cruising yachts today.

Savannah and *Borkumriff III*, on the other hand, have been designed to create the illusion of the past aided with modern engineering, structural materials, and sail-handling advantages. You would not envisage a schooner at the turn of the century having the sophistication of *Borkumriff*'s engine room, yet the interior and deck structures take you back to that time. What we all love about the 'classic yacht' is the visual comfort and grace produced and embellished by craftsmen. Whether I am working on a restoration or designing a 'new classic,' I am always trying to achieve that special feeling or spirit of tradition.

John Munford, Southampton, U.K.
Designer, Yacht Styling and Interiors

Ticonderoga (left), the 72-foot ketch designed by L. Francis Herreshoff and built in 1936, was the inspiration for the 92-foot Whitehawk, designed by Bruce King and built over forty years later. Choosing to recreate an aesethic and functional concept is truly a tribute to the enduring nature of classic design.